W9-DDO-929

WITHDRAWN

# COMPLETE
# PREMARITAL
# CONTRACTING

WITHDRAWN

# COMPLETE PREMARITAL CONTRACTING

## LOVING COMUNICATION FOR TODAY'S COUPLES

### JACQUELINE RICKARD

M. Evans and Company
New York

Copyright © 1991 by Jacqueline Rickard.

Originally published in hardcover as *Save Your Marriage Ahead of Time: Premarital Contracting—Loving Communication for Today's Couples*. First paperback edition copyright © 1993.

All rights reserved. No part of this book may be reproduced or transmitted in any form or by any means without the written permission of the publisher.

M. Evans and Company, Inc.
216 East 49th Street
New York, New York 10017

Library of Congress Cataloging-in-Publication Data

Rickard, Jacqueline.
    [Save your marriage ahead of time]
    Complete premarital contracting : loving communication for
today's couples / Jacqueline Rickard.
        p.      cm.
    Originally published under title: Save your marriage ahead of time.
    Includes bibliographical references.
    ISBN 0-87131-739-7 (paper) : $8.95
    1. Marriage—United States.   2. Antenuptial contracts—United
States.   3. Interpersonal communication.   I. Title
[HQ734.R536   1993]
646.7'8—dc20                                                        93-26893
                                                                        CIP

Sample clauses from chapter 9 and 10 copyright © by Matthew Bender & Co., Inc. and reprinted with permission from *Lindey on Separation Agreements and Antenuptial Contracts*.

The universality of the issues intimate partners face make the examples used in this book seem very familiar; however, all names and details have been changed to protect people's privacy.

Designed by Bernard Schleifer

Manufactured in the United States of America

9  8  7  6  5  4  3  2  1

To Bob—
For what we are together

# *Contents*

What was essential in the past may not be required now.

Lovers can determine what bygone rules live in their present marital expectations.


## Part II:   Intimate Communication

Partners can talk to and hear each other by using supportive premarital contracting and negotiation techniques.

Premarital Contracting encourages trust.

Contracting mates tell each other what they want and what they are willing to do. With the goal of having a loving relationship, they work toward joint resolutions for their individual requirements.

Contracting: A compelling form of communication between lovers.

Partners establish how their impending marriage will affect, satisfy, and fulfill both of them.

Couples face predictable themes of conflict.

Having worries to deal with is not terrible in itself. But leaving conflicts unresolved, allowing them to undermine your relationship, is.

## Part III: The Premarital Contracting Process

Lovers who know their goals can use covenants, Contract Law, and experts as resources; partners who contract will save their marriage ahead of time.

Contracting: Now and forever for your healthy, happy, ongoing marriage.

Premarital contracting need not end; it can become marital contracting.

Serve yourself.

The material included here and at the end of each chapter will support lovers searching for tools to find their own answers.

# Acknowledgments

*Save Your Marriage Ahead of Time* evolved out of my husband Bob's and my premarital quest to be clear to ourselves and with each other about our requirements in a loving way. Although we searched in bookstores and libraries, there were no books that offered appropriate guidance. We struggled to find a comfortable premarital contracting path on our own. While on our honeymoon, it occurred to me that there must be other couples who, while wanting to establish certain ground rules before they marry, wonder how to make their goals binding in a non-belligerent fashion. And so, this book was born.

To augment my premarital contracting experience, I interviewed many premarried and married couples. I am indebted to them for generously sharing their stories. Still, it is not enough for premarital couples to know what topics they might confront; loving contractors also need an array of possible solutions. Happily, all the experts I spoke with suggested helpful and practical alternatives for premarital couples to consider. On a personal level as well, Bob and I thank these professionals for their advice; support that we continue to use in our married life. My special appreciation goes to Trine Bech, Mel Frumkes, Irene Javors, Sylvia Law, Peggy Natiello, Grier Raggio, Jr., M. Dee Samuels, Ronald Schmucker, Marjorie Maguire Shultz, Richard Singer, Jr., Gary Skoloff, Martin Sobel, Nadine Taub, George Tierney, and George Van Sandt for their contributions to this book.

Ed Eastwood's willingness to work with Bob's and my conditions for creating a prenuptial agreement made our private association with the legal world a happy one. Patricia Barr's supportive responses to my premarital contracting ideas and her introductions to Family Law practitioners in far away places launched the book. I cannot thank my writer friends Carole Klein, Phyllis Goldman, Janet Dallet, Alex Fowler, Carolyn Latteier, and David Mathieson enough for their pithy comments and valuable suggestions. Janet Weinberg gave me the gift of her time to check my manuscript for clarity, and Neil Moss, caring brother and lawyer that he is, checked chapters nine and ten for possible legal misinterpretations.

Heartfelt thanks go to my editor, George de Kay at M. Evans and Company. His wise guidance forged the final shape of this book. A special acknowledgment goes to the National Conference of Commissioners on Uniform State Laws for giving their permission to include the *Uniform Premarital Agreement Act* in the appendix. My children Michael, Jonathan, and Lesley Shorr's belief in me enriches my writing and my life. My parents Rhea and Lou Moss's blessings give me great joy.

Without Bob's love, continual encouragement, and lucid reviews of each chapter as they first emerged from computer screen onto paper, I could not have finished this project.

JACQUELINE RICKARD

# Save Your Marriage Ahead Of Time

*With love, premarital contracting works.*

> Be prepared.
>
> SCOUTS' MOTTO

Are you afraid of getting married?

Have you avoided commitment because you don't want to be trapped?

Do you question the validity of the institution of marriage?

LYING FLAT on my back, left breast exposed for my yearly EKG exam, I listen as the doctor explains. He says, "My fiancee was so furious after I told her I wanted a prenuptial agreement that she wouldn't see me for three months." Quickly, our roles reverse. I am the expert, the doctor seeks advice. Like many other lovers, this young man is desperate for some guarantees before he marries.

Searching for security, frightened to commit to getting married without it, many people use prenuptial agreements as when-the-marriage-dies escapes. Couples circle their issues warily, keeping a safe distance from each other like wrestlers in a ring. Wanting to win but afraid of losing, they guard their individual goals rather than developing mutual solutions. Countless other lovers, feeling this kind of interaction to be too adversarial, yet without another solution, choose not to pledge wedding vows. Instead, they live together unmarried.

## *A glimmer of hope*

> Michael, a sculptor, and Maria, a watercolorist, have been living together very happily for a year. I visit with them in their art-filled, Greenwich Village studio. Now they are contemplating marriage and raising a family, but with great trepidation. They explain their fears. "We've seen what happens to our friends after they marry. Their relationships spoil." They ask, "How can we remain lovers once we are husband and wife?"
>
> Figures of high divorce rates pop up in the news often enough to push our panic buttons. Lovers mumble quietly to themselves, "Is it safe to marry?" "Why bother if it won't last." But even with all this turmoil and confusion, "Marriage continues to be the most popular voluntary institution in our society."[1] Still, Michael and Maria, like many others, are hesitant about their decision. So I ask them, "Why do you want to get married?" Michael answers, "We see marriage as our shared declaration of commitment to building a life together."

Yesterday's couples could rely on fixed, marital role models for guidance, but men's and women's expectations have changed too dramatically for past traditions to be enough for today's partners. Now, people of all ages and lifestyles are searching for ways to build relationships that have mutual respect and space for individual growth. What is the answer for lovers who want a marriage that will last through tomorrow's world?

---

1. David H. Olson, Ph.D.; "How Effective Is Marriage Preparation?"; David R. Mace, Ed.; *Prevention In Family Services: Approaches to Family Wellness*; Beverly Hills: Sage Publications, 1983; p. 65.

## Premarital contracting with love

Dr. Peggy Natiello says that contemporary couples who want to have a lasting relationship must "learn to address their issues of concern when they appear."[2] The not-so-secret formula: communication, negotiation, and collaboration between two people who trust each other. Dr. George Tierney advises premarital partners to "look at your concepts of marriage, and then learn about your mate's."[3] Supported by your love for one another, premarital contracting will profoundly strengthen your relationship.

## Only rich people need one

Premarital contracting is not just for Hollywood stars and business moguls who want to protect their assets as they whirl through "fantastical" life experiences, traveling from one divorce to the next. Contracting works for anyone who is interested in clarifying subjects not yet discussed, issues not yet resolved. Preparing a marriage covenant (whether in the form of a legal contract or a private statement just for the two of you) motivates lovers to learn about one another, expand their trust, or, perhaps, discover *before* they marry that their partnership has unsolvable problems.

This is contrary to the most frequent scenario presented by the media. The couple depicted is pitiful. The man, wealthy and terrified of losing his assets, frantically tries to guarantee their safety. Just hours before the wedding, he forces the woman he loves to sign a prenuptial agreement. Clearly, he thinks she is after his money. The heroine, successful in business, but less wealthy than her older lover, is driven by her need to get married and have children before her biological time clock runs down. The story ends; she is shocked that he doesn't trust her, but knows she will sign the abhorrent contract

2. Peggy Natiello, Ph.D. is an Adult Development consultant in private practice in New Jersey. She is the co-director of the Center for Interpersonal Growth in Port Jefferson, New York.

3. George P. Tierney, Ph.D. is a psychologist in private practice in New Jersey. He is Clinical Director of Parkway Counseling Associates in Rutherford, New Jersey.

because she does not want to lose the opportunity to marry and become a mother. Fade out.

Celluloid fantasy at its worst. Didn't this couple talk to each other before they agreed to marry? Why are they getting married? Is it to protect their assets, procreate, or, dare we imagine, could it be, to build a happy life together? The public has been misdirected into perceiving the prenuptial agreement only as a means to save assets in case of divorce.

### Premarital contracting is a positive process

Frequently, when people hear what the subject of this book is, they challenge me with the question, "Why only address divorce problems?" Many intimate partners still assume that prenuptial agreements mean only one thing: an aggressive defense in case of divorce. *Save Your Marriage Ahead of Time* announces that premarital contracting is a constructive communication process. Lovers can deal forthrightly with the distinctive factors that make up their partnership, and remain in love.

This book offers lovers two general types of premarital contracts: public legal contracts and private intimate contracts. Legally binding contracts (prenuptial agreements) are necessary for issues that need the backing of law in case of divorce *or widowhood*, as, for example, allocation of assets for children of prior marriages, or to safeguard the operation of a family-held business. Lovers also contract private agreements to resolve marital questions that family law will not intrude upon but that impact today's marriages, resolving such issues as how to share child-care duties, set up two-career couple's schedules, or clarify responsibilities for stepchildren.

### I knew that!

Contracting is not an unfamiliar, obscure technique; we use it daily to clarify our goals as we relate with business associates, family, and friends. By contracting we admit that we have conflicts of interest, but we agree that we will endeavor to resolve issues to our common benefit. So why is there resistance to premarital contracting? The romantic period of courtship, experts agree, is a state of being in which couples, intensely in love, ignore reality. Attorney Trine Bech, a Family Law practitioner in Hartland, Vermont, identified this syndrome as "the ARP: the Acute Romantic Phase." She warns her clients of its symptoms, "If you think your partner's underwear left in a pile on the floor is cute, you are still in the ARP. Beware!"

Typically, however, many lovers say, "We don't have problems. Even if we do, we can deal with them *after* we are married." But substitute the word "issues" for "problems" and most people will admit that they have some. Dr. Olson, observing the effects of the lack of premarital preparation, points out: couples "are often afraid to challenge or discuss issues because [they think that] this might threaten the partner and possibly become serious enough to end the relationship."[4] As your romantic relationship unfolds, you can contract about personal issues. Deciding jointly, for example, whose kids to spend Saturday with can set the stage for more intimate contracting. As your love matures, each contracting success encourages you to speak up about issues you are more emotionally invested in.

## Let's do it

There are determined couples who strive to communicate openly, trusting in the strength of their love. Jonathan, Katy, and I sit in a San Francisco cafe, celebrating their first wedding anniversary. They describe the hurdles they had to overcome during their ARP as they struggled to be straightforward with each other. Jonathan, straightening his tie and clearing his throat, begins, "I was afraid Katy would stop loving me if I told her my innermost needs. I knew some of them were different from what she expected; but she listened to what I said and didn't jump at me. My trust in her and in us grew as we talked things out." A smile spreads across Katy's face as she confirms, "We

---

4. Ibid., p. 67.

learned that by working issues out together, we could settle them for both of us."

## *May the force be with you*

How does preparing a prenuptial agreement help you further your relationship during your ARP?

> Rick and Lesley, in their thirties, are two-profession newlyweds. They see the contracting process as a force that encourages intimate communication. Looking relaxed in his warm-up sweats, Rick says, "It helped me to be more open because I knew that the contract, as a legal document, would hold us to what we agreed. I couldn't merely hope certain critical issues would not cause trouble, I was obliged to voice my concerns and we had to deal with them."
>
> Lesley, winding down after spending a long day at her office, continues their explanation, "The prenuptial agreement's inherent enforcement power freed me from my fear of being too aggressive if I spoke up for myself. I knew that I had to present what was important to me or I would be acquiescing to conditions I didn't want." Rick agreed with Lesley's admission that "our traditions had taught us that it was not right to be self-interested with the one you love." "But," he added, "we know we each have our own needs and requirements, and our contracting allows us to talk about them."

Premarital contracting will not simply produce a few economic controls; it is a process that can take you to the far reaches of your personal experience and to the center of your filled-with-wonder relationship. Attorney Grier Raggio envisions a marriage contract not only as an enforcer of conditions, but also as a framework of the couple's hopes, expectations, and goals. His advice to lovers is, "Save your marriage ahead of time."[5]

---

5. Grier H. Raggio, Jr., Esq., practices in New York City. He is the chairperson of the Marital Property Committee of the Family Law Section of the American Bar Association.

## Life's lessons

Having gone through a harrowingly emotional divorce I was terrified of marriage. Moreover, the marriages I observed around me were discouraging, not models of what I wanted for myself. Then a few years ago, I found myself in love with a man I knew was right for me. We wanted to get married. To be free to love my husband without fear of succumbing to my past expected roles I was determined to maintain responsibility for myself and vigorously participate in my life's decisions. Still, I knew that I needed strong support to maintain my convictions. For me, security came in the shape of a pre-marital contract.

Bob and I floundered about trying to find information about pre-nuptial agreements. Searching in libraries and stores, we could not find any books that gave constructive suggestions or positive ideas on how to make a loving contract. We contacted lawyers who readily gave us sample prenuptial agreements, but they were examples we knew we didn't want to follow. Slowly, we created our own intimate contracting methods. *Save Your Marriage Ahead of Time* is the result of our quests, our tribulations, and our accomplishments as we struggled to write our prenuptial agreement.

## This is not a how-to-be-your-own-lawyer recipe book

Instead, it is offered as a companion for couples trying to discuss who they are, what their expectations of marriage are, their fears, and their dreams. Living in a public world where win/lose attitudes reign, it is difficult to keep love reciprocal in our private lives. This book champions caring for both yourself and your mate.

## What's in the package?

The principle of *Save Your Marriage Ahead of Time* is that you are here to collect ideas, not prepackaged solutions. The book is divided into three main parts to bring you progressively to your own decisions.

## *Awareness

The first section presents the book's theme: premarital contracting builds loving marriages. It explains the historical evolution of the modern notion of marrying for love and illustrates such concepts as the Acute Romantic Phase, the benefits of contracting, and the dangers of choosing not to speak up about issues of concern.

## *Communication

The second section looks at communication styles, both gender-influenced and individual methods, and demonstrates contracting and negotiation techniques. To assist lovers in identifying their goals, this segment presents common issues of conflict, such as which assets are whose, work and child rearing arrangements, as well as other separate and joint responsibilities.

## *Process

The third part explores the use of contracts and the steps needed in their development and completion. Available support systems that couples can use as they create their premarital contracts are also examined.

For Bob and me, the most difficult factor as we tried to contract was deciding *where to begin* our discussions. To help you jump that hurdle, at the end of each chapter there are questions to use as idea stimulators and discussion launchers. How you communicate, as much as what you discuss, influences the results of your talks. It is essential to give your lover the background of why you respond in a particular way so that she can understand your viewpoint. As you work together to create your marriage structure, your "whys" will guide both of you to jointly resolve your issues.

## No pain, no gain

After lengthy, wonderful, difficult,and scary learning exchanges, Bob and I completed our legal and private premarital agreements.[6] More importantly, we developed a communication process that we expect to use throughout our marriage, one that encourages honest communication, respect, and caring for one another and ourselves. We discovered how empowering marital contracting can be. *Save Your Marriage Ahead of Time* will give you a concrete method of communication that allows you and your lover to uncover, discuss, and resolve your personal affairs. This process will support you as you work to build premarital rapport strengthened by mutual trust and love; gaining a partnership that will grow into a vibrant marriage.

### Where do we begin talking?

- Knowing the *whys* that influence your answers make you and your lover wise!

### Once you marry do you worry that:

- You won't be able to focus on your career?
- Your children from your prior marriage may lose what is rightfully theirs?
- You will have to sacrifice your independence?

Your *whys* make your lover wise!

---

6. See, "In This Troth Do We Pledge?" for an explanation of the types of agreements.

*When you and your partner discuss what you each want in your marriage:*

- Can you reach joint decisions?
- Do you only argue?
- Must you give in to your lover's wishes?

Your *Whys!*

*To begin your discussion session, pick a subject to talk about that gives you both joy:*

- What do you have the most fun doing together?

Your *Whys!*

# I

# PREMARITAL AWARENESS

Historical expectations, gender communication styles, and romantic notions of love almost always dominate premarital couples' relationships. With an awareness of how these forces influence them, lovers can use premarital contracting to create their own marital structure.

# PRENATAL
# AWARENESS

# 1 *Isn't it Romantic?*

*Draw aside the curtain of romance to
see your love.*

> Even if you're on the right track,
> you'll get run over if you just sit there.
>
> WILL ROGERS

Have you skirted money issues because you think they are too cold
and businesslike to bring up at such a happy time?

Do you avoid talking about your differences because you fear that
doing so would kill your romance?

Are you ducking the "how to's" and the "who will's", and, instead,
are you assuming that all will work out okay once you are married?

"I DON'T WANT TO talk about money now and ruin how happy we feel.
I'll wait until we're married; we can deal with it then," Jim says,
although he is very worried. He is not a shrinking violet, but a bank
officer who knows the need for preplanning in personal finance and
insists on it for his clients. Unfortunately, he does not take his own
advice.

The most common objection to premarital contracting is that by
revealing monetary concerns or other anxieties to your lover you may
cool romantic passions. Therapist Irene Javors cautions couples, "As

long as people are afraid to air what they think and feel, they are not going to ask their lovers questions that may be very relevant to whether or not they want to marry."[1] Problems that remain unresolved may cool more than passion; they can destroy the relationship.

### *There are costs to being silent*

The assumption that romantic feelings are fragile and should be protected above all else is self defeating. Danger lurks in this kind of logic, so a dilemma exists: fear of losing the excitement of romance, yet very much not wanting to make a grave mistake. Although we may choose not to act on it, most of us sense that information gathered by talking honestly with our lover is protection against disaster.

> Haden, a pediatrician, listens to my explanation of premarital contracting as a positive method of communication, and is unconvinced. Wearing an elegant, red silk dress protected by a white coat, her stethoscope hugging her neck, she exudes professional expertise. She sits at her desk, her forehead furrowed, and her hands moving restlessly through piles of patients' charts. Staring at the wall behind me, Haden explains her concern, "Mitch's family is very religious. I'm afraid that his mother is going to insist that I change my religion so that I will bring up her grandchildren in their faith. Although I'm prepared to raise my children according to my in-laws' wishes, I won't convert because that would hurt my parents. I'm worried about how this will affect Mitch and me." Quickly she adds, "I don't want to talk about it with him now. It could get too explosive and spoil this grand passion we feel. We'll work things out when the time comes."

When-the-time comes is the most difficult place to begin discussing issues that are laden with intense emotions, for that is when we are pushed to our limits and crowded by the events that forced the crisis in the first place. There are so many latent traps inherent in Mitch

---

1. Irene Javors is a psychotherapist in New York City. She specializes in gender and relationship issues.

and Haden's circumstances that it is difficult to imagine them not talking about their potential predicaments ahead of time.

Javors says, "We are struggling against a cultural view of story-book romance. The whole issue is about communication. But we have a screwed-up notion about relationships: that if you are in love you don't need to talk anything through; it will all come out right on its own. This Hollywood notion of love is the first step toward divorce."

### *Questioning leads to discovery; it is a method of learning, not destruction*

"I can't ask him about that!" Susan exclaimed, worried about whether Tim, her soon-to-be second husband, minds that her son will be living with them. "Tim would think I don't have confidence in his love." Tim had agreed to this arrangement, but the two of them never fully discussed how Susan's eleven year old son Jesse would fit into their new life together. Talking openly about Jesse would ease the pressure for Tim and Susan as they establish their new stepfamily. They sure have a lot to discuss. How does Susan expect Tim to be involved in Jesse's upbringing? Is Tim concerned that Jesse might intrude on his and Susan's time for intimacy? Is Susan uncomfortable bringing Tim into her son's world?

### *Talking frankly about trouble spots ahead of time gives reference points for the future*

A fantasy that is dangerous for intimate partners to believe is that we should not ask questions of our lover because it signifies lack of trust. Susan and Tim will face many day-to-day occurrences with Jesse that could strain their love. To insure their freedom to say what has to be said at the moment of showdown, they have to make clear to each other what their overall attitudes regarding Jesse are. Then, without fear of misunderstanding or recrimination, when Tim and Jesse have a disagreement there can be a more natural flow of reactions and resolutions. Susan, knowing how Tim feels in general about her son, won't invest extra heavy meanings in his interactions with Jesse.

Although we cannot foresee every problem we will encounter with our lover and decide our solutions in advance, by talking together about issues before they confront us, we can come to general understandings of our motives. Then, we can avoid making emotional assumptions in the future.

## Lifting the curtain of romance

Romance is fragile, much too ethereal to maintain a marriage by itself. What is it after all? Dictionaries define the state of romance as, "without a basis in fact, fanciful, fictitious, or fabulous." It is a time of "idealizing one's beloved." Romance is part of falling in love, but love cannot survive on romance alone. Devotion has to be fed and cared for. What better way to nurture your love for each other than by being genuine and honest? While it surrounds you, coloring everything, your fresh love can inspire you to be giving and compassionate as you and your partner identify your expectations of marriage. Develop options at this gentle, romantic time rather than when you are embroiled in a predicament.

## Once bitten, twice shy

Confidence and trust in your partner will grow as your relationship evolves. Most of us carefully measure out our trust to new friends and business acquaintances. Often though, we give trust too quickly to our lover. Earning trust is an ongoing process, and the ARP is a wonderful time for intimate partners to develop faith in each other. As your trust in one another increases, your mutual commitment to your relationship will flourish.

Dan and Sheila describe how, while they created their premarital agreement, their trust in one another grew. Sheila explains,

"Years earlier, when I was going through my divorce, I had a long battle over child support." Through court intervention she had received subsistence level maintenance, but that was all. "Fortunately, my parents supported me while I struggled to build a career and make enough money for my children and myself." It had taken Sheila many years and hard work before she achieved her independence.

Dan had been divorced as well, but without the kind of stress Sheila had. Scarred by her experience, Sheila was insistent that she keep all of her income and assets separate from Dan's. He says, "My immediate reaction was to interpret her needs as a judgment of me rather than a response to her past. I felt terribly hurt." But Sheila's economic hardships had been so traumatic that, as she explains, "I knew the only way I could feel comfortable enough to marry Dan was to insist on my separate security. I needed control over my possessions."

During their discussions, which lasted months because of their combustibility, Sheila's fears were dispelled as Dan acknowledged her requirements. With his ARP-colored vision, he could focus more on her needs than his; and with help from an accountant who dispassionately explained Sheila's financial picture and suggested alternatives, they agreed on a plan.

Sheila says, "Slowly, because of how we contracted, I gained confidence in myself and trust in Dan. The outcome of their premarital contracting surprised them both. While Sheila would keep her assets separate—thus fulfilling her need to know that she could survive on her own if life came to that—she offered to pool her income with Dan's. Elated, he recognized that Sheila's commitment to their relationship was as strong as her drive to protect herself.

### Okay, you are convinced, but how do you do it?

You read this book in hopes of finding recommendations so that you can avoid living with unresolved worries. Prenuptial agreements might already have been suggested, but they seem scheming solutions, not loving arrangements. My husband Bob describes the sample agreements we received from some lawyers when we began our search for contracting models as, "divorce-decrees-made-in-advance." Those examples frightened us so much that we didn't do any more thinking about our premarital contracting for weeks.

## What not to do

The most offensive example was a prenuptial contract written for a two-profession couple. It identified who would pay for what clear down to their toothpaste. The document itself had more pages dedicated to termination of their marriage than clarification of marital issues. There were no indications of the partners investing in their relationship. Giving and sharing were missing. The couple did not seem in love, instead they appeared terrified of marriage. There was no evidence in their agreement of any commitment to the future of their relationship.

## What to do? What to do?

If you are like Bob and I were, you don't want to create a divorce-decree-in-advance contract. Sure we had statements we wanted to make, but positively and with compassion. Still, the question of risk came up again and again, "What will such talking do to the romance of our love?" Many of us have convinced ourselves to be silent rather than speak frankly about concerns that really bother us. I certainly had in my past. It can be terrifying to face the thought that your lover might respond in a way that would cause an argument, or worse, a breakup. Yet issues are issues *because* of their emotional importance to us, and they are not easily ignored.

Memories of a bitter divorce motivated me to speak up. Your reasons to be open about your needs may not be as easy to listen to, and the resistance to disturbing your romance may be more difficult to challenge. But it can be done, and the results are well worth the struggle. By communicating your goals and values, you may not avoid all marital pitfalls, but you will be aware before the fact which problems might surface. You will have talked about them while the glow of romance sweetens your explanations, reactions, and responses.

## Surprise benefit of marital contracting

In our premarital contracting, I could talk frankly with Bob thanks to his support of my goal of making a legal contract, and our mutual desire to avoid divorce. The result was more than both of us expected: a deeper sense of our love. Although certain issues turned out to be very touchy for us (finances and household responsibilities were our nemeses) and our discussions were frequently emotional, by listening to each other, over time we created arrangements that we could commit to.

Also, addressing everyday issues that were easier to face, whose brand of toothpaste to buy (we now get both of our brands) or who does which meal chores, we learned how to contract together about more serious concerns that we had to face. Our successes further cemented our belief in us as a couple. "This is great!" Bob said. "We can deal with our problems. I don't have to ignore them." He had also gone through a divorce and valued this difference.

What really surprised me was that I cherished the way Bob showed his anger. He didn't try to force me to accept his view. Bob spoke quietly, even if not always calmly, and he tried to convince me with reason, not histrionics. We were learning how each of us reacted in touchy situations, and how to respond to each other without feeling destructively defensive or angry. The process of creating our legal prenuptial agreement became more valuable than the actual document itself, because we were developing skills that we could use throughout our marriage.

## *A not so secret method of success*

Of course there was stress for Bob and me as there most likely will be for you. The chapters on communication offer suggestions about how to handle tense situations. One technique that helps us ease into the discussion of an emotional issue is to begin the session with a subject we both enjoy. For us, it was talking about our future goals. By contemplating our hopes and plans, we felt that we were already building our life together. This encouragement gave us the impetus and fortitude to wade through our more difficult target subject of the day.

## *Meet reality through clarification*

Expected marital obligations and responsibilities, of yourself as well as your lover, must be explored to keep love alive and growing. Javors observes, "Many women are terrified of losing their autonomy, of getting sucked into a traditional way of life. There are men who don't want all the traditional burdens, but unless the roles are clarified, there is no point of reference for their interaction." When you have consciously chosen your marital responsibilities, and your partner selects hers as well, you both are less likely to be angry or resentful.

Bob and I, during a visit to Port Townsend, Washington, relax in a Victorian inn's cozily furnished drawing room. We chat with a young couple. Bill and Cara are on their first vacation since Josh was born. It is the last week of their child-care leaves of absence from their jobs. They work in the computer industry: Bill as a systems designer; Cara trains software users. During the weekend, we have observed how each of them handle the baby with love and ease. Obviously, they both have been intimately involved with Josh.

Our conversation turns to the subject of my book, and as often happens when the topic of premarital contracting comes up, people give the gift of their personal experiences. Bill, cuddling their two-month-old, describes how he responded when Cara insisted on a premarital agreement, "She had lived on her own for six years and hadn't ever been in a long-term relationship. She let me know that for her to marry me, specifics about our daily living had to be defined. I told her I would help out; Cara wanted to know how. That didn't bother me because I felt strongly that for our marriage to work she had to be comfortable."

Josh fusses and starts to cry. Bill walks away, soothing and rocking their boy. Cara, smiling at his retreating figure, remembers, "My friends thought I was bitchy. It was real hard for me to speak up. I had to though, because I wanted to make it clear to him which things I wanted in our marriage and which I didn't." Bill returns with Josh sleeping in his arms. He says, "I wrote my objectives for our marital contract. They were values that I strongly believed in; for example, I wanted our focus in this marriage to be our mutual growth."

"His thoughts were beautiful and very important to me," says Cara, describing her reaction, "but I also wanted concrete statements about everyday functions. It wasn't that I didn't trust him, I just had to know where he stood. We developed our lists trying not to get too heavy about everything. Bill, kidding, included the stipulation that we load the toilet paper feeding out over the edge of the roll, not from under it. But we covered a lot of important points, like how we wanted to raise our kids."

### It is not easy to make this choice

Premarital contracting can be scary. Javors explains, "When you start premarital communication you are really bringing to the surface questions about what people's conceptions of love are, and what their criteria are for caring. It can be really frightening because suddenly you are confronting the mystery of love. I think most people are very reluctant to do that." Bob's and my premarital contracting helped us discover in real terms what we were willing to do because of our love. Sometimes, however, people do not want to confront how little they, or their partner, give in a relationship.

Working out who writes the checks, how you will share household chores (and they are never finished, even if you hire cleaning help), who shops for dinner, or any of the myriad of daily interactions above and beyond your separate existences are opportunities to build trust. Why assume that a conflict means an end? Truly it can be the first step to agreement and more feelings of love.

## Speak up now or forever hold your peace!

Often declared at traditional marriage ceremonies, now or never is an ominous message. Speaking up before the marriage ceremony rather than waiting until after is a very wise move, made doubly wise by continuing your dialogue throughout marriage. Premarital contracting disentangles your expectations from the glitter of fantasy; by examining them, you will get the sense of whether your relationship is realistic or not. Continuing to contract after you are married keeps your union whole.

Attorney M. Dee Samuels reflects, "People always ask divorce attorneys why marriages fail. Their simple answers, when I redirect the question back to them, may be, 'Oh I changed and my mate didn't,' or 'I grew out of the relationship.' Those are the symptoms maybe, but I don't think they're the reasons. Lack of communication is really what happens. I think that is what brings people into my office."[2] When you communicate, you and your sweetheart connect with your minds. As long as you talk to each other and give out information, solutions can be found. Lack of communication breeds assumptions; and worse, if you do not explain what bothers you, or what frustrates you, you are choosing to keep malevolent vapors in your relationship.

---

2. M. Dee Samuels, Esq., of San Francisco, California, is a Certified Family Law Specialist. She is on the Council of the Family Law Section of the American Bar Association, and has written and lectured widely in Family Law.

## *Love makes the world go round*

Love is incredibly powerful. It causes us to try what ordinarily we would never consider possible. While we have it, we believe that love is forever. Yet it never ceases to surprise me when people choose not to talk about concerns because they fear that to do so would destroy their special relationship. If they believe that their love is so fragile, how can they justify their faith in it? Ignorance is not bliss, it is a time bomb waiting to explode.

### *Where do we begin talking this time?*

Knowing the *whys* that influence your answers make you and your lover wise!

- How can you make sure that getting married is the right decision for you?
- How do you define love?
- Are you being as careful about your marriage as you are with your career, clothes, or choice of books to read?
- Do you know how your mate will respond to issues that are important to you?
- Are you romanticizing your partner?
- How committed to this relationship are you?

Your *Whys* make your lover wise!

### *To begin your discussion session, pick a subject to talk about that gives you both joy:*

- Describe one of your favorite hopes.

Your *Whys!*

For those of you who would like to read more about the subject of this chapter, the following books are suggested:

*Getting The Love You Want: A Guide For Couples,* Harville Hendrix
*Love Is Never Enough,* Aaron T. Beck, M.D.
*Love Isn't Always Easy: a Collection of Poems on Love and Making It Work
. . . Because It's Worth It,* Edited by Susan Polis Schutz

# 2 Who Said Marriage Had To Be This Way?

*What was essential in the past may not be required now.*

> If we do not know our own history, we are doomed to live it as though it were our private faith.
>
> HANNAH ARENDT

Has your concept of marriage come from the past or present?

Whose values do you use to measure your lover?

Have you and your partner created your ways of interacting, or have they been predetermined by others?

GARY, a struggling artist, is losing his tolerance. "Because Patti pulls in a great deal more money than I do, her friends always tease me, calling me a 'kept' man. They're not the only ones; I feel guilty that I'm living off her." Patti's friends, Gary, and all of us dance to old time tunes. Men who break the conventional mold and marry women who earn more money than they do, or who are higher up on the professional ladder, face a great deal of social and private censure. Women pushing traditional boundaries also must defy intimidating hurdles.

## *Wherever did we get these ideas?*

Marital patterns formed centuries ago for needs that no longer exist are still alive and kicking in most of us. They have been passed along in many ways: within the home, through laws, and by social mores. Although change has begun, "Our current laws concerning marriage, divorce, alimony, and custody were taken en masse from English common law, some of which is more than five hundred years old."[1] Glorified romance, still promoted on television, in movies and advertisements, shapes our expectations. And even as we announce belligerently to ourselves, "I will never behave in my marriage the way they do in theirs," we reproduce our parents' patterns. If we want to actively participate in the design of our intimate relationship, we cannot lose sight of the influences that shape our courtship and marriage. But I wonder, when today's lovers leap, how much of their initial, almost unconscious attraction for each other is inspired by messages from the past. We can satisfy others: family, friends, bosses, or ghosts; or we can choose to fulfill ourselves.

## *Traps of traditional responsibilities*

The current breakdown of historic gender roles and responsibilities has caused confusion and pain to us as individuals and as members of a society grappling with contradictions. In order for lovers to see clearly what they want in marriage they must be conscious of old-fashioned controls as they meet current opportunities.

## *Newfangled concept encounters old control #1
The 'What is mine is yours, what is yours is mine' philosophy of the past meets the 'What's mine is mine' generation.

Historically, most husbands and wives had a simple contract that presumed a 'forever' marriage. It went this way: the husband provided

---

1. William J. Lederer, and Don D. Jackson, M.D.; *The Mirages of Marriage;* W. W. Norton & Company, Inc.; New York; 1968; Norton paperback; 1990; pp. 14–15.

the wherewithal for survival, the wife was the caretaker of their daily needs. Mostly unspoken, this agreement nonetheless functioned for centuries. Today, the various options of lifestyles available to couples, plus the menace of divorce, have neutralized that conventional contract. Sad to say, engaged couples who straddle the past and the present break rules in both camps.

Glenda, a stunning young woman wearing her shoulder-length blond hair intricately braided, slowly turns her gold bracelet with her long, red fingernails. She looks cool, but inside she is boiling. "I'm done with Frank. He's too selfish for words. I could never rely on him again." With a logic based on her social conditioning, Glenda expects her man to provide for her. When her fiance, Frank, a newly trained dentist, insisted on a prenuptial agreement to safeguard his future earnings in case they divorce, she broke their engagement.

When I had met with Frank a week earlier, he told me proudly that his fiancee was a high-fashion model. His smile faded as he added, "It's such a competitive field that there's no way she'll make a good living." He announced stubbornly, "I love her, but I've got to protect myself."

Glenda, with strong conviction, says, "If he really loved me, he'd want to take care of me." Frank, with an equal sense of being right, is convinced that she is going after his money, not him, "or she would sign the prenuptial agreement my lawyer wrote up for us." Caught up in their particular historical rules, these angry lovers are not listening to each other's fears. By demanding instead of communicating, they lose the opportunity to create new policies and keep their love.

### *Newfangled concept encounters old control #2
### Is home only where the Mom is, or are Mom and Dad both there?

Barbara, a vice president at a large commercial bank, ponders why, "now that I am a mother, I don't have as much power of concentration at my office as I used to." She finds herself thinking about Richard, Jr. How is he doing at school? Will he be infected by the current outbreak of chicken pox? Sitting in her office, she is distracted by concerns that are too far away.

Five years ago Barbara was the youngest vice president at her bank, but now her star seems to have fizzled. She says, "I'm emotionally exhausted by the conflict of career pressure and mommy demands. No matter which way I turn, I feel guilty and frustrated." Her husband, Richard, describes the integration of parenthood into his life, "I can focus on my work more than my wife says she can. I don't always have Richie in the back of my mind. I just assume things are okay. Having a child really hasn't changed my life much." Although they had agreed to raise their son together, this couple yielded to a traditional pattern: the child is the woman's responsibility. If Richard helps at home, it is to assist Barbara rather than as her parenting partner.

Many modern women, while contributing to the financial support of their family, are, nevertheless, unable to insist that their men participate in the housework and child rearing as partners. They are trapped in the belief that the family is the woman's obligation, and men seem to agree. According to a recent poll taken by *The New York Times*,[2] 17 percent of the women questioned, between the ages of eighteen and twenty-nine, thought that the most important problem faced by women today was the conflict between work and family or childcare. Interestingly, only 9 percent of their male peers recognized this dilemma. Such a sizeable disparity warns premarital couples that not discussing how their family will function may lead to disaster.

### Ancient customs

Prenuptial contracts were powerful tools in the world of antiquity. Early contractors had clear goals: definition of property boundaries,

---

2. Linda Belkin; "Bars to Equality of Sexes Seen as Eroding, Slowly"; *The New York Times*; August 20, 1989; pp. 1 & 16.

economic protection, and spousal responsibilities. Generally, women had no control over their own wealth; they relied on their fathers and then their husbands for security.

It is difficult for me to imagine what life must have been like for women who were not allowed to be responsible for their possessions. But, in fact, it was not until the mid-nineteenth century that the "Married Women's Property Acts" were passed to protect American wives from losing their legal existence, "abolishing common-law restrictions on their right to contract, sue and be sued, and acquire, hold, and convey property in their own right free from interference by their husbands."[3] It is easy to understand the inner struggle many women still have to speak up for what they want. History's instructions to women was "Be silent!" to keep in the good graces of their men; fathers, brothers, and spouses held the reins of control over their security.

### *What may have sufficed before, hinders us now*

Our conduct continues to be judged by ingrained biases. Men are expected to strive for success in terms of money and power. Those who choose different standards are presumed strange and weak. Women are supposed to have their men make the responsible decisions; those who don't defer are labeled as too strong and selfish. Lovers can decide how they want to be.

### *Current contracts mirror the past, but do they reflect the present?*

### *Cohabitation agreements

Lovers living together before marriage, an arrangement that has recently become socially acceptable, also have a link with antiquity.

---

3. *American Jurisprudence*, Second Edition; Volume 41, Section 17 "Married Women's Acts"; The Lawyers Co-operative Publishing Company; Rochester, N.Y.; Bancroft-Whitney Company; San Francisco; 1968; p. 30.

In Scotland, there was a tradition called "hand fasting" in which a couple, holding hands, verbally committed to live together for a year and a day before marrying. The partners agreed that if they did not marry, "and if the woman became pregnant, whoever of the two had decided to dissolve the relationship was obliged to take responsibility for the child."[4]

Contemporary couples who choose to cohabit rather than marry, perhaps because the marriage commitment causes discomfort or is legally unavailable to them, will have, even if unspoken, contractual commitments. The question is, as in any partnership, what has been agreed to? Without coming to terms on such important issues as lifestyle or finances, you have elected not to be caring for yourself. See chapter "But Why a Legal Contract?" for a discussion on how, by not contracting, you have agreed to stipulations set by law. It is important for partners living together to realize that cohabitation agreements, like premarital contracts, can be positive tools of communication.

## *Kettubahs

Ancient Jewish marital contracts, called "kettubahs," spelled out and guaranteed the "obligations and rights of both parties."[5] Today, kettubahs are again included in many marriage ceremonies, and they are legally binding contracts. They express the attitudes of the signers, some having basically the same language as those written centuries before, others personalized to fit contemporary alternatives. A third attitude exists: one lawyer I interviewed confided to me that he and his wife, also an attorney, had signed a kettubah aware that they did not know its conditions. The contract was written in Hebrew, but that was not their reason. "We were afraid we'd open a Pandora's box so close to the wedding. It was easier not to question." Lawyers are human too.

4. "Courtship Rituals"; *Ms. Magazine*; November, 1987; p. 27.
Jonathan Gathorne-Hardy in *Marriage, Love, Sex and Divorce*; (Summit Books, New York; 1981) dates one year's trial marriage in Scotland as occurring until the time of the Reformation. p. 16.
5. Helen Latner; *Your Jewish Wedding*, Doubleday & Company, Inc.; New York; 1985; p. 17.

Today's couples have requirements for protection that are similar to those that our ancestors had when they entered their prenuptial agreements, but our criteria are compounded by emotional issues not addressed in earlier times. Although divorce statistics have made the value of premarital agreements evident, our complex motivations dare us to create such a document. Many couples decide to look the other way.

## *Begin with your personal history*

With marital boundaries so open to a couple's interpretation and so removed from those of just a generation ago, it is incredibly difficult for individuals to verbalize, let alone contract for, the specific factors uniquely important to them. Not having role models to supply vocabulary and illustrations of what we want, it becomes almost impossible to describe our goals to ourselves. How can we explain clearly such amorphous aspirations as personal fulfillment and individual recognition?

Struggling through a divorce in the early seventies, I was shaken loose from my classic fifties background. While I concentrated on bringing up my children as a single parent for fifteen years, I raised myself as well. I had to do a lot of archeological digging: sifting through my history, delicately examining its shards, and keeping what was valuable for me. Finally standing on my own, I reached the place of knowing my capabilities as an individual.

Because of a hardy strain of self-doubt and a lack of confidence in the institution of marriage as I knew it, I had decided never to marry again. Like many other best laid plans, when Bob and I fell in love my resolve to stay single was swept away. But my heritage haunted me. Could I keep my hard-won identity, or would I succumb to my memories of "shoulds"? I had identified my old patterns, but I wasn't convinced that I could keep them where I wanted them, out of my marriage. It was paramount for me to contract with Bob about how we wanted to be, even though we had been relating that way all during our courtship. We agreed to use the structure of a premarital agreement to help us sustain the focus of our communication.

Although the final draft of our legal contract contained very little of the lifestyle declarations we struggled to clarify (they had been edited out on advice of counsel), they remained a private covenant between us. It did not matter whether our statements were enshrined in a document that would hold up in court. We had spoken out about our dreams for our new marital dynamics and our fears of our past conditioning, and had come to a mutual understanding. I was keeping my history where I wanted it, in my past.

## *I think I know my history, but what is yours?*

It is important for men and women to acknowledge their partner's past too. Attorney Patricia Barr,[6] working to break the barriers of gender bias in her state's courts, explains, "The woman is coming from the position of disadvantage assigned to her by history, culture, and environment. At marriage, the woman ought to take extra care in structuring her position in the union as opposed to the position history has handed to her." Men face readjustment headaches also. To enjoy the benefits of the new love and work styles, they must give up some of their ritual bastions of power.

As Gary, whose story began this chapter, said, "When I think of a married couple, I see three parts: the you, the me, and the us. Each relationship may blend in different proportions, but all those components are necessary." The "I"s do not have it.

## *Change is scary*

"The truth is that change has as much to do with endings as new beginnings. Any important change demands that we leave behind a

---

6. Patricia Barr is a senior partner in the law firm of Barr, Sternberg & Moss in Bennington, Vermont.

relatively comfortable and predictable way of being."[7] And our personal history sure is familiar. Not surprisingly, even when we find certain behavior of our lover's or our own painful, that it is known and predictable often makes living with it seem safer than stepping into the unknown of change.

### Can love survive wedded bliss?

While in the ecstasy of the Acute Romantic Phase, most of us are very giving and understanding. We are intent on watching what happens between us and our lover, how we each act and react. We strive to communicate and be responsive to one another. Also, we know some of what we do not want to do: perhaps not to act like our parents did, nor relate the way we did in our first marriage or in earlier relationships. But for many couples, something switches off after they settle into their wedded state. Repeatedly, I have been asked—what is in the institution of marriage that causes the love and happiness a couple has before they marry to drastically change? A friend gave me a pithy answer, "Because 'wife' means possession and 'husband' means ownership."

It is more complicated than my bitter friend's explanation. Once we are committed in marriage and lulled by its historical promise of "now and forever," the intense awareness of self, present while we are going through courtship rituals, fades. With that loss of self knowledge, our perception powers atrophy. Old rules and regulations that were dormant during the ARP seep up from the deep recesses of our memories. Archaic gender roles and behavior patterns surface and the modern person you are is also a carrier of teachings of the past.

### There is a whole new world out there

"Until a generation ago there was a social consensus as to what marriage meant."[8] Then, as conventional marriages cracked apart, there

---

7. Drs. Melvin Kinder and Connell Cowan; *Husbands And Wives: Exploding Marital Myths/ Deepening Love and Desire*; Clarkson N. Potter, Inc., Publisher; 1989; p. 64.
8. Marjorie Maguire Shultz, Esq.; "Contractual Ordering of Marriage: A New Model for

were battles to keep the traditional order. Fortunately, the resulting divorce statistics hit us over the head and screamed, "Take notice." The result is that, albeit slowly, in many social and legal arenas new marital structures are being recognized and embraced. Special solutions for each couple are there for the taking, but require a conscious effort by lovers to reconcile conflicts inherent in their old and new expectations.

### *Premarital contracting is a positive communication process that can assist you and your lover to clarify your relationship*

Now that the marriage structure is not rigidly controlled by our society, the question is not whether, but how to discuss marital dynamics. Lovers must unlock the hold their history has over them. Only then is the door open to their personal choices.

#### *Where do we begin talking this time?*
The *whys* of your answers make your lover wise!

- Does your lover fit or break traditional expectations?
- What you-should-do's do you want to keep out of your relationship?
- How will your marriage be different from your parents'?
- When you don't agree with your partner, do you speak up for yourself?
- When you express your concerns do you feel guilty? Too aggressive? Pleased?
- Do you want your lover to speak up for himself?

#### *To begin your discussion session, pick a subject to talk about that gives you both joy:*

- What traditions have you and your mate created?

State Policy"; *California Law Review*; Boalt Hall School of Law, University of California, Berkeley; Vol. 70, No. 2; March 1982; p. 207.

For those of you who would like additional reading on the subject of this chapter, the following books are suggested:

*The Future of Marriage,* Jessie Bernard
*The Marriage Contract,* Lenore J. Weitzman
*The Mirages of Marriage*, William J. Lederer and Don D. Jackson, M.D.
*Writing A Woman's Life*, Carolyn G. Heilbrun

# II

# INTIMATE COMMUNICATION

Using constructive premarital contracting to support intimate communication and caring negotiation techniques in their search for answers, partners can talk to and hear each other.

# 3 Is Hot Love A Cold Business?

*Premarital Contracting encourages trust.*

> It takes two to speak the truth—one to speak, and another to hear.
>
> HENRY DAVID THOREAU

Do you think love brings freedom from conflicts?

Can you stand up for your rights with everyone but your lover?

Are you the boss at home?

BURT is a self-made man. "I have always," he told me proudly, "gone straight for what I want. When Rita and I were getting married, I wanted to make sure that if we divorced she would not get my money. I had a contract drawn up by my lawyer, and then had Rita go to his office to read it. I told her 'Sign it or we don't get married.'"

When I interviewed Rita, she confides with regret in her voice, "I gave up some pride in myself at his lawyer's office. I knew then and I know now that I would walk away from his money if our marriage ever broke up. I've been on my own since I was eighteen and I can fend for myself. But I couldn't speak up." By signing Burt's one-sided prenuptial agreement without responding to his implied message, Rita didn't let him see who she was, and they both lost an opportunity to build trust in one another. Premarital contracting can give you and your mate valuable information if you both participate in the process.

## *Individual contracting is not a mysterious process*

We contract every day. When you and a friend discuss which movie to go to, you are contracting. Lovers, sitting comfortably at dinner on a Friday night, discuss where to go for their hike; that is also contracting. The contracting process is simple: identify the goal, determine its benefits, face its consequences, and then formulate options from which to select a joint decision.

Premarital contracting allows you and your lover to reach mutual aspirations. Sure, prenuptial agreements are a great tool to establish legal protection for your children born of a prior marriage or to establish your marital property distribution. But intimate contracting also works for settling issues as small as how both of you will help prepare tonight's meal or who will be first to use the shower this morning; arrangements that reflect how two lovers respect one another.

## *Contracting with your lover*

Whether creating legal prenuptial agreements or personal covenants, loving couples employ the same intimate contracting skills. Unlike the way we may contract with business associates, strangers, and friends, mates need not juggle for an advantageous position over each other. Instead, we can reveal ourselves, expressing our fears and emotions as well as our hopes and goals. Love brings two strong new influences to contracting: a willingness to be especially caring, generous, and supportive to our partner; but also, an overwhelming sense of vulnerability. Comments that your lover makes, ones that had they been made by friends or co-workers would normally slide off your back, stick like glue. Your throbbing heart responds, "How could he say that and still love me?" or, "If she really loved me she wouldn't want to do that." There must be a fundamental commitment between lovers who encourage open exchanges to treat each other with compassion.

## *Speaking up makes your life easier*

Disclosing your feelings, expectations, and fears—speaking up—is far less dangerous than what you might face if you keep silent. "It doesn't really matter how patient, knowledgeable, well intentioned, or kind either [partner] is, or whether they are Ph.D.'s in psychology or spiritual saints. The estrangement and anger will grow to the extent that there is an actor reactor imbalance, so that one feels primarily responsible and the other feels primarily controlled."[1] With each of you contracting for yourself and expecting your partner to do likewise, you both are actively involved in building a loving, functional relationship.

## *Conflicts of interest between partners do surface*

A myth that many of us believe is that your love is suspect if you and your mate disagree. Must we like, agree, want, or dislike whatever our lover does? No two people can continuously have the same desires. Partners are two wholes, not a combined single entity. Intimate contracting encourages lovers to clarify their authenticity to one another, and to themselves.

If your communication is supported by mutual commitment to your relationship, it is geared for success. A businessman can always go elsewhere to buy supplies or make a deal. Friends leave to go to their homes. But lovers want to stay together, so they have to learn how to deal with issues that arise or their conflicts will tear their partnership apart. Dr. Natiello says, "Emphasis in those relationships is on openness, on individual contracts that can be

---

1. Herb Goldberg, Ph.D.; *The New Male Female Relationship*; William Morrow and Company, Inc.; New York; 1983; p. 52.

renegotiated, on the potential for transformation for both partners within the relationship."[2]


## Premarital contracting: negotiate, don't compromise

Intimate contracting is based on the premise that lovers understand that each partner has equally important interests to be considered. It is not an act of compromise. One partner does not have "to weaken or give up (one's principles, ideals)."[3] Connie, a woman in her forties, is in the beginning of a new relationship. Struggling to break a habit that has caused the downfall of her other relationships, she tells me, "I was the one who always said, 'All right! Let's do it your way.' Not anymore. I know I'm important too."

When we compromise, we give up recognition of our own value and become angry. We resent our mate's selfishness, whether we accuse him silently or out loud. On the other hand, if our partner compromises, we may be the recipient of his resentment. Contrary to compromise, negotiation honors the concept that it is natural for two sides to have disparate views. For Connie and other contracting partners, negotiation is a process in which the two lovers "confer, bargain, or discuss with a view to reaching an agreement."[4] The sustaining motivation in premarital contracting is that both of you are working toward joint resolution, not merely trying to satisfy your individual needs.


## Contracting works

When you speak up about what you want, you will feel strong because you have taken care of yourself. Knowing that your lover gives serious thought to your view, you will feel loved because you

---

2. Dr. Peggy Natiello; "Men/Women Issues In Human Development" (Private Circulation); p. 15.

3. *Webster's New World Dictionary,* Second College Edition; Prentice Hall Press; Cleveland; 1986; p. 292.

4. Ibid., p. 952.

are recognized. When you listen to your partner's side, you will feel kind because you are caring. By resolving the issue at hand, you will feel effective because you are successful. Working with your partner to create a mutually satisfactory solution, you will feel exhilarated because you have connected.

Nichole and Ben have been living together for six months. Wanting to feel secure in their individual worlds first, they are planning to marry next September after both have been in their present jobs for three years. In their late twenties, they have demanding careers. Ben, after completing his Masters in Science, became a high school teacher. He spends most of his after-class hours having conferences with students, coaching seasonal sports, and preparing lesson plans. At school before 8:00 A.M., Ben often doesn't come home till after 8:00 in the evening. Nichole, an accountant, is working her way up the executive ladder of a medium sized company. Her schedule is as rigorous as Ben's.

It is Saturday afternoon and the three of us sit around their dining room table completing our interview. Nichole and Ben describe how, that very morning, they had avoided a potential conflict: how to get ready for their guests. Two couples are coming to their apartment tonight for dinner. Typically, Nichole thinks their place has to be cleaned; Ben is usually convinced that it is neat enough. Their contracting process began when Nichole realized that she wanted Ben to participate in completing *her* goal. She wanted the living room, dining area, kitchen, bathroom, and their bedroom straightened up.

## *Premarital Contracting: Present your goal

Lovers can give information clearly and in a positive, non-threatening manner. Instead of sideswiping and blaming, hoping to motivate her partner through intimidation, Nichole says to Ben, "It is important to me that the house be clean tonight. I'd like your help." She knew that she wanted to contract a solution, not engage in a fight. Ben carries with him a dislike of housecleaning and a readiness to put off any chores for the minutest of reasons. But, since he wanted to have company and was aware that in their relationship that requires pitching in, he engaged in constructive contracting with Nichole. He tells me, "I didn't think the apartment looked so bad, and I know that I'd rather sit surrounded with disarray than clean up. But I also know Nichole needs to have everything organized."

## *Premarital Contracting: Discuss possibilities

Nichole and Ben exchanged ideas until they hit on an arrangement that was good enough for both of them. It took just a few moments for them to arrive at their solution. Ben says, "We agreed to split the cleaning and not to do the bedroom." Each felt their decision was satisfactory, and they were ready to work for the immediate goal of getting their home in shape for their guests. Ben honored Nichole's discomfort with having an untidy home; Nichole respected Ben's dislike of cleaning. They had given recognition to themselves and one another, and to the importance of their relationship.

Nichole and Ben have honed their premarital contracting skills into effective communication tools, but in the early commitment stage of their relationship their arguments didn't go so smoothly. Afraid of conflict, they waited until their emotions reached explosive levels, but the cost was too great. They began speaking up sooner and learned that disagreements do not have to be battles; they can be healthy clearinghouses for troublesome issues. Anger, rational discussion, pain, intense revelations, humor, and love weave in and out of wholesome fights. It is all right to express human emotions when we are dealing with issues that are very important. But if we can have discussions supported by contracting techniques that help us keep focused on our goals, agreement between partners is achievable.

## Successful premarital contracting

Here are some hints to assist partners in their premarital contracting communication:

*Hint #1: Work with, not against your differences.* Each gender has been trained to use different strengths; attributes that we could, if we allow ourselves, embrace, enjoy seeing in our lover, and respect. In a discussion, many men want to concentrate on the specific facts; a lot of women want to address the attendant feelings. These attitudes are essential to positive contracting; each can be valued by both partners. .

Bob and I have different body rhythms that could have caused us problems when we moved to the Northwest and changed our lifestyle. He is a slow starter in the morning; I move fast. Back east, Bob had a long daily commute, so he left the house by 6:45 every morning. In order for him to leave on time and since he liked to slowly build up to the pace of his day, we awakened very early. While Bob meandered through his ritual of dressing, I, done with my preparation, could go downstairs and have a quiet cup of coffee. Thanks to Bob's commute schedule demands, I was at my desk by 7:00 A.M.

But in our new world, when we began to schedule the work day, our opposite rhythms had the potential for serious conflict. Bob doesn't have an hour and a half commute anymore. He only has to go downstairs to his office, so we get up later. My discomfort with our new schedule was caused by the fact that once we began our day, Bob still took his time, whereas I wanted to get going and start my writing.

Using our marital contracting techniques, which incorporate Bob's logical approach and my awareness of emotional factors, we worked on our individual goals for our daily timetable. Instead of trying to blame or change each other, we resolved our dilemma. Now, I complete my early morning responsibilities before breakfast while he dresses. Bob does his chores after we eat, while I go to my desk. We meet in the middle for breakfast and we enjoy being together. He moves at his pace; I zip along at mine. We have created a mutually satisfactory contract.

*Hint #2: Lack of clarity costs us.* Fear that by speaking up we may alienate our lover adds to the hesitation many of us wrestle with as we try to be candid. But by not stating straightforwardly what we hope to accomplish, our mate, confused, senses a threat. When we are in danger, most of us react with self-protective vigilance; we may protect ourselves by becoming defensively aggressive or silently resistant. These shields can compound the problem we are trying to solve because they change our joint communication style from one of give and take to a wary, escalating struggle.

The immediate repercussion of not contracting is that there will be no cooperative settlement that both of you can adhere to and benefit from. In the long term, the conflict spirals and spreads causing more and more infectious damage to your love. Those gyrations will lead you and your mate to a relationship filled with resentment, anger, and finally, hate.

*Hint #3: You don't have to do it their way.* Understanding your lover means just that: understanding. You are not locked into agreeing with what she wants. Communication that is supported with an awareness of your lover's experiences and prior training encourages you to empathize with her struggles. Additionally, knowing that your partner considers your side as well helps you act less defensively. You and your mate's intimate talks will help you disengage from your personal traditions and build new methods of interaction. As a result, you will be more loving to each other, and more willing to work out mutual solutions.

*Hint #4: Life is not perfect.* Many of us think that when all does not go well, we are at fault. The very act of confronting problems means facing that we have them. Although we cannot make life turn out just the way we want it to, it is in our control to acknowledge that problems turn up, and that when they do we will not deny them. With our lovers we can talk about what we would like to happen and what we can do to better existing conditions. We can contract and reach solutions.

## Intimate contracting comes in handy

There are bound to be rough spots in your relationship that surface regularly, and they can be smoothed with communication. Do we split this dinner, or are you paying for it? This Sunday, are we going to go on a hike together or are you off to see your parents—and must I come too? For each decision to be made, contracting is the method of choice. Many daily issues can be resolved in the flow of the moment. But time and again, there will be predicaments that need serious contracting to be resolved. By maintaining an adaptable routine of contracting so that you both participate in solving your less traumatic encounters, you will evolve communication patterns to rely on when you have to wrestle with big decisions. At those stressful times you can concentrate on the subject since the means of communication between you and your mate will have become second nature.

## Your presentation influences the outcome

Contracting is a complex interaction. Just as a ballet performance is more graceful the better qualified its dancers, the more negotiating skills that you acquire the better your premarital contracting will be. All of us can master constructive styles of communication if we want to. The first step in acquiring effective negotiating skills is evaluating your current tools. Search through your personal style of communication and evaluate your methods. Do your techniques get you what you really want?

Our gender conditioning contributes to the communication techniques we use. There is a "crucial distinction between the female search for feminine identity through intimacy and the male search for masculine identity through achievement."[5] You can choose your techniques. Reaching for intimacy with your lover does not mean you have to give up your side of the issue; striving for personal achievement does not mean you must dismiss your lover's reasons. It is possible to negotiate with your mate despite divergent male/female approaches, but it requires a continual awareness. Are your current communication styles assisting you when you contract with your mate, or are they barriers to reaching agreement? For successful contracting we must know which of our techniques are effective.

## *Technique one: Be up front

Once you have decided that you want to contract about a concern of yours, let your mate know in as neutral a manner as possible what the subject is. If possible, give your partner that information prior to getting together to discuss your issue. By alerting your lover to the topic ahead of time, instead of just announcing, "We've got to talk after work!" you can alleviate his worrying, "What have I done wrong?" More importantly, you allow him time to think about the information you have given him.

## *Technique two: Where and when

When you expect to do serious contracting, establish a time and place. The location will help set the ambiance of the scene; selecting a future time gives each of you space to think in the present.

Actual time: not too late, nor too early. Nichole tells me, "In the beginning of our relationship, I remember Ben and I having a ridiculous argument about whether my being too tired was a valid reason not to have a discussion."

Place: choose a favorite spot where you both can be relaxed.

---

5. Ethel S. Person; "Some Differences Between Men and Women"; *The Atlantic Monthly*; March 1988; p. 72.

Protect yourself from being intruded upon by phone calls. Cultivate an atmosphere that supports your contracting; have a favorite record or tape playing softly in the background. At night set out candles to soften the mood.

## *Technique three: Keep your eye on the shell

Don't wander; stay on the subject that caused you to call the meeting. It is important not to use this discussion as a springboard to check off a laundry list of accusations that will escalate into such clever retorts as, "Oh yeah, well you did . . ." If you bring in tangential elements, so will your lover. This clouds your contracting session's focus and distracts you and your mate from achieving your goal. Remember, you want to create a mutually acceptable resolution for a particular obstacle.

## *Technique four: You can call "Time out!"

If you or your partner is really uncomfortable during the discussion and would like to stop the meeting, that is okay. But before you do, affirm that the problem remains to be worked through. Things do not go away because they are ignored; they stick around. If you can, set up a time to talk again. Taking a ten minute break, or a day or two of rest, can be very beneficial. A respite allows you and your partner to mull over what you both have said. It gives each of you time to move away from your discomfort and be less defensive and more flexible. When you call for an intermission you are not being hostile, you are taking a breather.

Nichole and Ben remember one heady month their first winter together when each had tremendous pressure put on them by their jobs. Both felt strained to their limits. Nichole recalls, "One night I came home much later than I had planned. Exhausted, I hoped Ben would be there and see how tired I was. I fantasized that he would insist on drawing a bath for me and not let me do anything but relax. Of course, Ben wasn't even home yet."

"When I staggered in an hour later," Ben says, "I wanted sympathy, but Nichole was lost in a dark gloom. It didn't take me long to join her mood, nor did it take much time after that for us to fight over something. Finally, we just said 'no talking now.'" They learned the value of taking ten.

## *Technique five: Confirm past successes

One of the most effective ways to begin your constructive contracting is to open the session with an affirmation. Chatting about an earlier solution that went well, or each of you giving one reason why you are happy to be together helps set a positive mood for your discussion.

## *Technique six: Anticipate joint resolution

It is important to approach a premarital contracting session with the expectation of reaching a win/win solution, rather than hoping to sway your lover to do it your way. While you are in the learning stages of premarital contracting, have the confidence that the exuberance of your ARP will support and fortify your aspiration to be loving and kind to your partner.

### *Ready; get set; come out running!*

While you are new at intimate contracting, you and your mate can inspire each other for encouragement. Start the session by validating the reasons you are there. Pledge your commitment to your relationship and to your goal of working together to reach an agreement that satisfies both of you. It is important to review your rules and routines for the discussion session. Reaffirm the constraints you established during earlier contracting, such as agreeing not to interrupt each other and not to criticize. Moreover, you and your mate can confirm your willingness to be supportive and flexible. Promise to restate what your lover has said so that you make sure you have understood him correctly, and commit to not taking too long to explain your side of the issue.

Develop your contracting techniques; add conditions that make you feel comfortable and take away methods that cramp your style. Trust in yourself and your partner. Remember how you worked through your last problem. Was the situation cleared up immediately, or did it take a while to reach agreement? Don't expect the impossible.

## Premarital contracting delivers

We lovers need all the help we can get to keep our most precious relationship alive. Premarital contracting gets us on the right track; continued intimate contracting keeps us there. Some gifts lovers get from their intimate contracting are:

*Gift #1: Premarital contracting encourages partners to be respectful of each other's boundaries.* Your needs are significant to your lover simply because they are yours. Caring recognition by your partner encourages you to do the same for him in return. This nourishing action and circular reaction generates its own positive energy. Your trust in yourself flourishes because you can be your own advocate. Trust flows from you toward your lover as you witness how he accepts and respects you. Once you have learned that your mate will not hit below your emotional belt, instead of using up energy to defensively hide your vulnerabilities, you can support his needs with compassion.

Anne and I met at a friend's house. We quickly reached a point in our conversation where we recognized a mutual interest: marital contracting. After recounting to Anne the thesis of my book, she told me her story.

"When Matt and I first were together, Saturdays went like this: lazy time in the morning, breakfast around 11:00 A.M. I would have preferred to get up early, exercise, eat, do a couple of washes, and have us both get the cleaning out of the way by that time, but I couldn't bring myself to say so. Instead, the slow pace continued as we sat around reading and eating, perhaps starting some work around the house by 3:00 P.M. By 10:00 that evening, Matt would be ready to call it quits. I, meanwhile, had conked out on the couch hours ago.

Anne and Matt began to see through their ARP curtain after they lived together a few months. Anne says, "The promise of our weekends didn't always fulfill our dreams. I'm a morning person; he is a late starter. I wind down early, he is wired for hours longer. Matt was slightly aware that I was uncomfortable and not really enjoying our relaxation time. But I couldn't express my discomfort, even though I felt it. We were in love. How could I want to do something other than have romantic weekend mornings? It took months of this routine for me to realize that it was my responsibility to ease the frustrations that were caused by disregarding my needs.

"I told Matt my thoughts and he explained his to me. He relished lounging around after a week of work. We had to look into what we each wanted, how we each worked, and who we were. It was a terrific strain to keep from being judgmental or trying to make one another change.

"We tried getting up early, but he felt pressured and uncomfortable. After many reshuffles of the available options, we came up with our solution: one early morning and one late. Usually, Sunday was the early day. That way Matt could count on Saturday for his wind down day. I could tolerate Saturday's late rising routine because I knew we would be up early Sunday. Also, I realized that if I felt the need (and very often I did) to get up and do some active project on Saturday, it didn't cause any disharmony between us.

This experience gave Anne a love-building message: Matt did not get angry with her when she chose to do what she wanted; he respected her boundaries. On the other hand, because she had taken care of her needs, Anne could respond to Matt's requests as kindly as he had to hers.

*Gift #2: Intimate contracting gives mates the power to steer together through the many channels their relationship will travel.* "When we fail to admit and affirm our own responsibility for all our experiences, and blame or acclaim another, we are giving away our freedom to change ourselves and to control our experiences."[6] When you are contracting, if you can be generous to your partner as well as be sympathetic to yourself you will succeed.

*Gift #3: Contracting helps set the ground rules so that you can accomplish what you want.* Unresolved issues foment anger and resentment that will attach to other situations as they arise. Intimate contracting offers an interactive framework that helps lovers get what they want—a solution for the current issue and moving on with life.

## Contracting works

Instead of expecting your lover to look out for your interests, when both of you take responsibility for yourselves, you will achieve mutual solutions. Ben says it well, "What you get out of this contracting is an understanding of your partner and how she will act in real gut issues. You each negotiate from your own position." If you and your lover go into premarital contracting with the idea that there is something in it for each of you, both of you will win.

### Where do we begin talking this time?
The *whys* of your answers make your lover wise!

• Do you like the way you and your lover deal with conflicts?

---

6. I found this quote, attributed to the Yogi Amuh Desai Krualu, posted on a friend's refrigerator.

- How do you respond when your partner tells you what he wants?
- What is your most ineffective communication technique?
- What contracting techniques would you like your mate to use?
- What is hardest about intimate contracting?
- Are you trustworthy?

*To begin your discussion session, pick a subject to talk about that gives you both joy:*

- What do you love about the way your lover expresses herself?

For those of you who would like to do some additional reading on the subject presented in this chapter:

*People Skills*, Robert Bolton, Ph.D.
*The New Male Female Relationship*, Herb Goldberg, Ph.D.
*Dreams of Love and Fateful Encounters: The Power of Romantic Passion*, Ethel Spector Person
*Ways of Being Together*, Michael and Nina Shandler

# 4 What's In It For Me?

*Contracting: A compelling form of communication between lovers.*

> Where love reigns, there is no will to power; and where the will to power is paramount, love is lacking.
>
> CARL G. JUNG

When something bothers you, do you feel helpless or furious?

Does true love mean that you and your lover must want the same things?

Are you afraid that your marriage will change your life for the worse?

"MELISSA is so engrossed with her research and her friends in the program that I feel totally left out of her life. Weekends are dreadful. That's when we could relax together, go to a movie, have some fun. Instead, I spend most of my weekend doing work around the house; she's always at the library. Will we ever have common interests again?" Phil's complaints will be familiar to those couples in which at least one partner is involved in some form of career training. He continues, "Without her salary, the drain on my income is intense. When is this going to end? I don't resent her getting additional education, but I feel our connection is fading. What's worse is that we can't discuss what to do about it without fighting." This is not just Phil's problem; it is Melissa's too.

### Solve or dissolve

Premarital contracting can help Melissa and Phil deal with their impasse. Working together to create solutions that nurture their love, they can satisfy their separate needs too. By listening as well as speaking up, they can differentiate between the circumstances that they have little control over, but that nonetheless influence their lives, and their personal choices.

### Self-interest nourishes; selfish acts destroy

It is hard, though, for many lovers to get beyond the misleading myth that states, "It is selfish to speak up for yourself." Unfortunately, the difference between acting in one's own interest and being selfish is difficult for many of us to distinguish. Selfish acts are those you do for yourself without regard for others. Stating clearly what you want is not in itself a selfish act. You can pay attention to your interests and still not violate your lover's.

### Contracting brings peace of mind

The premarital contracting process, with the give and take inherent in its structure, allows you and your mate to take care of individual needs. By doing so, you both will have more energy for each other.

### *Successful Contracting: Think of your lover as well as yourself

Frank fell in love, and panicked. Wanting to protect his furniture store from being devoured by a possible divorce decree at some later time, Frank had his lawyer draw up a prenuptial agreement that would have his fiancee Tara sign away any future spousal interest in the store. Tara was crushed when she read the document. She felt that Frank didn't trust her, lacked confidence that their coming marriage would last, and was inconsiderate of any children they might have. She felt that he had very little commitment to make their relationship work. His prenuptial agreement quickly became a cause for fierce arguments between them and they broke off their engagement.

## *Successful Contracting: Don't beat around the bush

If you are trying to protect your assets in case of divorce or death, it is important to tell your partner so. How you defend your resources, though, reveals a great deal about yourself, and what kind of interaction your partner can expect in the future. Guarding your interests without considering your mate's circumstances as well is one extreme pattern of behavior. Not speaking up at all for what you want is another. There are moderate alternatives for you and your partner that can lead to prudent asset protection solutions.

## *Successful Contracting: Travel the middle road; it has room for both of you

States do have general policies regarding distribution of marital and individual assets. But the courts allow couples to determine their own distribution program so long as the solutions are reasonable. Still, it is not sound policy if one partner gets nothing. If you and your mate arrange a property dispersal in your premarital agreement that markedly oppresses[1] one of you, the court may not enforce it.

---

1. Henry Campbell Black, M.A.; *Black's Law Dictionary*; Abridged Fifth Edition; West Publishing Company; St. Paul, Minnesota; 1983; Basic test of the unconscionability of a contract. P. 792 Chapter "What Makes A Contract A Contract?" and chapter "Your Premarital Agreement" discuss the legal requirements of a contract.

Attorney Richard Singer[2] suggests that couples look for fair and reasonable options when they prepare a prenuptial agreement to protect their assets. He advises clients, "Create a fund in lieu of equitable distribution." Singer explains the purpose for that arrangement, "I can put together an agreement in which your fiancee gets nothing. But you can't take it to court ten years from now and be sure that a judge wouldn't say that in good conscience they cannot enforce that agreement."

Singer suggests an alternative, "Instead of awarding an interest in the business to his spouse, the man promises that he will put a certain dollar figure into a trust fund until the interest earned and his continued contributions have accumulated an agreed upon total dollar amount. At that point he will have no further obligation to contribute to the trust. The fund will be the wife's property in case of divorce." This is a parallel construction solution, good for the wife and good for the husband. The protection of one spouse's assets is counterbalanced by the fund created to protect the other spouse.

## What's in it for us?

If both of you begin your intimate contracting dialogues with the idea that you will get something out of them, you will. Ben and Nichole, whom we encountered contracting about their housecleaning chores in the chapter "Is Hot Love A Cold Business?" help explain what can be gained from the premarital contracting process. "Our relationship was strengthened when we talked about real things and saw what each of us did with that information. I don't have to put walls up between the two of us with 'what is she going to take away from me?' worries. Instead, I can concentrate on coming up with creative ideas."

---

2. Richard H. Singer, Jr., specializes in Family Law. He is a partner in the New Jersey law firm of Skoloff & Wolfe.

## *I love you; you love me*

Surrounding the premarital contract discussions you have with your mate is the love you have for one another. Your commitment to those feelings will inspire you to generous action as you strive to reach specific agreements. When you are contracting you do not have to agree with one another's points to prove your love. Trusting in yourselves, you can build the inner strength to straightforwardly express your feelings and hear your partner's as well. Solutions won't always evenly satisfy both of you. There will be times when one of you is more giving to the other, but in time, the reverse will also be true. You don't have to deny what is important to yourselves in this process, and together you can look for new ways of attaining what you each want.

## *Premarital contracting strategies*

Can we speak up on our own behalf for emotionally charged concerns such as how to maintain our marital and separate assets, or how to share joint expenses if we don't talk about the less potent daily issues our relationship encounters? Being open and clear about our goals requires communication skills; premarital contracting strategies provide support.

## *Contracting Strategy: Think before you speak

To determine how you want to explain your concern to your mate in the premarital contracting session, you need to know what you want to say ahead of time. Identify your goal to yourself. If you aren't sure of what you want to accomplish, you cannot be effective in your contracting dialogue. The way you present your thoughts on an issue is as important as your intent. Moreover, the way you initiate your premarital contracting will influence the mood and tenor of the conversation.

## *Contracting Strategy: Talk straight

Sometimes, while we are trying to be compassionate for our partner's sake or because of our own hesitations, we blur the edges of our requests. Unfortunately, by not being clear we may give confusing information. For example, lovers often find it difficult to talk straight about money issues. Because of the power money has, financial issues are frequently laced with symbolic undertones. Some people use money as security, others wield it like a weapon. Many of us respond to money with a complex mixture of emotions.

Susan, a travel agent, and Mark, a landscaper, are both in their thirties. They are in the process of negotiating their premarital contract. Susan's body clock is ticking faster and faster, so she and Mark want to begin a family within a year after they marry. "But," she says, "for us to bring up even one child will cost a lot of money. I want a baby, but I want us to be financially secure too."

Mark is a shy, reserved, hulk of a man who loves buying woodworking tools, many of which cost hundreds of dollars. Susan, an outgoing, friendly person, is very willing to talk about their concerns. She explains, "I want us to have a budget that focuses on saving money." For the first year of their relationship the glow of their ARP had kept their divergent money-related attitudes from causing stress. But with marriage in the offing and newly formed joint plans, their separate philosophies cause disruptions in their contracting.

Mark and Susan's initial premarital contracting conversations about finances were unclear and usually ended with both feeling frustrated and angry. Trying to be gentle with each other, they did not precisely define their viewpoints on money. The facts are clear. Susan wants to save money; Mark collects special woodworking tools. They both have genuine reasons for their goals. Susan's is to save for the baby's expenses, and Mark enjoys working with wood. But their money discussions were vague because of misguided concerns. Susan did not want to be too pushy. Mark was concerned that she would think he was selfish. Their kid-glove treatment of each other barred both of them from being direct. Yet their goals were in jeopardy because of their conflicts.

The turning point for Susan came just a week before I met them, when Mark, happy and excited, had called her at the travel agency to tell her that he had gotten a great deal on a used lathe from a coworker. Immediately, Susan was overcome by waves of anxiety. "I felt the clock ticking away; there wasn't much time to save, and we needed all the money we could put away." She tried to keep in mind the pleasure Mark got from using his treasures, but it was hard not to think only of her anxiety. Fortunately, by the time they both came home she had calmed down. This time she was determined to have a productive conversation with Mark that would settle the brewing conflict.

Money is one of the most emotionally threatening subjects partners have to deal with. Lovers, confused, may try to avoid talking about money issues in a direct fashion. But subtlety doesn't work; it impedes you and your partner from discussing your real concerns. Partners need to be aware of their differences if they want to achieve mutual agreement.

## *Contracting Strategy: Make your point in a constructive way

So that your mate doesn't have to put up defenses, focus on the issue, not the person.

Mark, Susan, and I are sitting on their apartment's balcony, framed by wisteria vines. Warmed by the sun, the flowers' fragrance surrounds us announcing that spring is here. Susan and Mark are taking turns relating last week's contracting. Susan had begun her explanation to Mark with an inoffensive but true observation, "You and I have different ways we look at money." Mark explains how her comments affected him, "I was on the alert while I listened to her, but I didn't feel attacked. She was saying what we both know."

## *Contracting Strategy: State your feelings without blame

Your feelings are valid; you do not need to support them by accusing your partner of causing them.

> Susan had told Mark, "I get very nervous spending large amounts of money. It makes me feel like we are losing any chance of saving." Mark takes a sip of his iced tea, nods in agreement to Susan and me, and adds, "I didn't know where she was going with this, but I waited to hear more because her voice did not sound hurt or angry; it was calm."

## *Contracting Strategy: State your goal, but offer suggestions rather than dictating actions

Have confidence that what you want to do will get done. It is not necessary to be a dictator. Each of you can participate in coming up with an acceptable solution.

> Susan told Mark, "I would like to work out an arrangement so that your need to buy tools and my need to save are satisfied." She had gone on to explain her idea to Mark. "Let's work on a budget that includes both a saving plan and spending money for each of us."

## *Contracting Strategy: After you have expressed your views, leave time for your mate to think

Yes, you are trying to have your partner agree with your point. But using force doesn't convince, it only wears your mate down. To respond effectively takes effort. Give your lover space to think so that he can come up with his view of the issue.

Mark tells Susan, "I understand what you want to do. Although I don't feel as concerned about saving money, I want to make you comfortable. I need some time to let this settle in." Mark remembers how they felt after that exchange, "This was a volatile subject for us and we sure knew enough had been said. It was time to quit for the day, but we agreed to meet again Sunday after lunch. By then, we each promised to have a list of suggestions."

Sometimes, in one's fear of not being heard, we run over our partner, cramming our statements with more information and emotion than is needed. We can speak slowly and quietly, and still be effective.

## *Premarital contracting skills are a long-term investment*

Throughout life we will face conflicts, but with perseverance we can resolve a good many of them. Intimate couples who engage in active premarital contracting gain skills that they can always use. That is good news because life is filled with decisions, the results of which may always be present. One commitment that will, before and after it is made, give partners a great deal to talk about is having children.

## *Children are a life-long responsibility

Deciding how to raise children is always a challenge for parents. Dealing daily with discipline, guidance, or simply the need for a parent's presence, is not easy. We can add to that historic difficulty the knowledge that family structures are in a state of flux. Now, women have more responsibilities piled on top of their homemaking assignments. "Sixty-five percent of women with children under 18 were in the labor force in 1987, including 53 percent of women with children under 3 years of age."[3] Today, the traditional family model of

---

3. Diane Hughes and Ellen Galinsky; "Relationships Between Job Characteristics: Work/Family Interference and Marital Outcomes"; Bank Street College Of Education; New York; 1988; p. 3.

working husband and housewife "make up less than 10 percent of all families."[4] With parenting no longer clearly defined, child-rearing decisions demand constant reevaluation. To establish your family dynamics, mutual priorities must be set. One of the most common issues regarding children is their care.

## *Is child care one of your priorities?

It is important when you and your mate contract through your child-care options that you remember the different perspectives men and women have, even though some of those views may be changing. It is a fairly recent societal development for women to seek an identity through their careers, although this is a familiar drive to many men. Men and women value the work world, but they have mixed feelings about commitment to a family. The business world and our social framework have not particularly reshaped the way they rate the importance of child care—a mainstay of a woman's identity in the past. Socially, men who choose to be the primary parent are considered a little weird and unmasculine; women who opt to stay home with their children are judged to have no ambition. Companies penalize staff members, men or women, who choose to spend time with their family rather than to work overtime. Partnership opportunities are lost, promotions pass dedicated parents by, and coworkers look askance at such preferences.

Even as mates struggle with their differing parental values, joint efforts to come to workable solutions help their partnership. Encouragingly, a 1983 study "found that husbands and wives were more likely to be satisfied with their marriages if they perceived their spouses as doing more than their fair share of child care and housework, regardless of the actual time spent in such tasks."[5] In other words, your trying counts. The premarital contracting process gives

---

4. Ibid., p. 3
5. S. Yogev, and S. Brett; "Patterns of work and family involvement among single and dual earner couples: Two competing analytical approaches"; Washington, D.C.; Office of Naval Research. Quoted in *Balancing Work and Family Life: Research and Corporate Application* by Diane Hughes and Ellen Galinsky; Research Division, Bank Street College; 1988; p. 11.

lovers a structure to face issues together, discuss them from both perspectives, and create solutions as they need them.

## *Your intimate contracting techniques produce the result*

Most of us realize that if we want to get into good physical shape, we must exercise. We understand that to increase our strength we have to learn new training skills so that we can carefully build our muscles without damaging our bodies. This is also true when it comes to improving your communication muscles. Although we may recognize that our contracting skills need strengthening, it takes effort to reach the level of communication that we seek. Watch out for self-destructive methods that may keep you from improving your premarital contracting.

## *It's your fault: The Aggressive Method

Business contracting has given the contracting process an adversarial image: win at any cost; competition rather than cooperation. But that is not what intimate contracting is about. Arguing vehemently for your point, interrupting your partner's explanation, shouting your lover down, storming out of the room, or utter disregard of your partner's feelings and needs are actions that will destroy your message. Battle scars conquering lovers bear include loss of friendship, mutual caring, and intimacy. You do not have to overpower your mate to be effective.

## *No, it's my fault: The Giving-in Method

Not standing up for your values, acting powerless, blaming yourself, or not letting your partner know what you want are self-defeating techniques. Many women have been trained to believe the myth that being submissive is loving. Such action invites aggressive behavior from partners. An "Oh I don't know, what do you want to do?"

response is fine occasionally. We don't always have to have an opinion or a desire. Sometimes, what our lover wants to do is the deciding factor. But as a routinely held attitude, "Whatever you want," is not productive for either you or your partner. Not expressing your desires does not translate into being nice; it simply means you aren't being.

## *I exist, you don't: The Paranoia Method

Sometimes we are so afraid of not being heard or that our reasons won't count, that we can't stop to hear our mate. Miscommunication and defensive responses go round and round, and instead of looking for answers together, we get hooked on whose side wins. A useful premarital contracting technique that assures your partner that he is being heard is to repeat his point before stating yours. As well, this may help you understand his reasons better. Another technique that stimulates the communication flow is to refrain from interrupting your partner's explanation. Be patient; your turn will come. To make the waiting easier in the future, you and your mate can institute a constructive contracting rule: keep explanations short.

### *Trust and intimacy between partners increase with premarital contracting*

The achievements of your contracting are a direct consequence of the trust and intimacy you are willing to venture into with your partner. Some of us need to build up trust before we can reveal ourselves; others trust first and ask questions later. Whichever way we have been in our past most of us have experienced painful repercussions, but successful premarital contracting needs trust. By both of you taking part in premarital contracting, you can build mutual trust realistically based on one another's actions.

It is indispensable to intimate communication that each partner's emotions and sensitivities be acknowledged. Feelings will not be denied. If they aren't alleviated in one way, they leak out somewhere else. Your emotions, whether they stem from feeling threatened, overwhelmed, tired, frustrated, or gloriously happy, help you and your partner determine which solution will resolve the issue you are confronting.

## Stop trying to control all fronts

Many of us believe that it is our mandate to make things right. By attempting to control all outcomes we make pledges to ourselves and our lovers that we cannot keep. To ourselves we promise, "If I act just right, he won't feel insecure," or "If I can keep her happy, we won't ever fight." To our partner we promise, "I won't ever lose my temper again." Forget it, you don't have that kind of godlike power.

If you commit to what is neither possible nor true to your character, you are making a shaky contract. It would be better for each of you to learn what you cannot do, instead of exacting unfulfillable promises. "Will he still love me?" or "Does she want me after this?" are questions that can only be satisfied by real experiences, not by false pretenses. Know for your mutual benefit what you are willing to do and what goes against your nature. It is self-delusion to think that if you agree to something you are uncomfortable doing, you will be happy in the relationship. How you live is up to you. Each of you can learn to be flexible, creating options rather than succumbing to the temptation of promising too much.

## Premarital contracting gives us insights into our relationship

While you and your lover contract, you both become wiser.

## *Insight: Your strengths and your partner's are balanced

Although partners may not be equal in their strengths and capabilities, they are equal in their importance to the relationship.

Jessica, a bookkeeper for a few local small businesses, took on the responsibility of organizing her and Martin's finances. Marty, good at synthesizing ideas, was very helpful streamlining their solutions. Jessica's suggestions were backed by her accounting expertise. She is not more powerful than Marty because of her knowledge, nor is he more influential than Jessica because of his ability to see things logically. Their separate skills influence their joint actions. As well as similarities, partners bring varied attitudes and abilities to a relationship. Those differences keep their relationship vibrant.

◀ WISDOM: It is okay for you and your lover to speak up for yourselves. Both of you are important.

## *Insight: I appreciate my partner

Trying to intimidate your mate to obtain approval of your ideas, or passively wishing that your partner will choose your suggestions over hers are extremes to avoid. When we express ourselves so that our mate can hear what we say, we have successfully learned to respect our own strengths. To keep the cycle of intimate contracting rolling, we must hear our partner's response as well—a feat that is sometimes difficult to do in personal relationships. When your lover disagrees with you, it is dangerously easy to assume that it is because she thinks you are wrong. Unfortunately, judgment labels can lead lovers into defensive arguments. You and your mate have different perspectives; it is not that you are wrong and she is right.

When Jessica is not dressed for business, she is famous among her friends for the vibrating color splurges she weaves into her daily costume. Today, her clothes are no exception: purples, oranges, reds, and greens send out pulsating rhythms. But Jessica has a calm about her that comes from having confidence in herself and trust in Marty's respect for her. As their interaction about budgeting reveals, she also validates his importance, "Marty, how can we get the budget in shape enough to satisfy me and yet not be burdensome for you?" He sees that Jessica acknowledges his side of the situation as much as hers, and explains to me how that encourages his willingness to talk things out. "Jessica's support of me makes it easy to let go of thinking my idea is the only one. It helps me be open to hers too. Our regard for each other's needs frees us to decide together what we will do."

◀ WISDOM: Premarital contracting recognizes that conflicts exist between mates, but that does not mean they don't love one another.

## *Insight: Respect yourself

Denying your importance makes you angry with yourself as well as with those around you. Valuing yourself makes you feel good. Since most people will respond to you as you expect to be treated, your self-value gives an important message. If you belittle yourself, others will join in that chorus. Respect your boundaries and those around you will too. "Whether people feel loved and respected . . . are the two most important dimensions in marital happiness."[6]

◀ WISDOM: Your premarital contracting, motivated by interest in your own well-being, elicits love and respect from and for your partner.

## *Insight: Premarital contracting confirms our commitment to each other without handcuffing us together

Responding to your lover's concerns does not require that you must give in and relegate your wishes to the garbage. Nor do you have to feel guilty when you stand firm for what you want to accomplish. On the other hand, when you and your partner are trying to resolve how to reach your goals, you do not have to be rigidly invested in

---

6. Dr. John Gottman, a psychologist at the University of Washington, is quoted by Daniel Goleman; "Study Defines Major Sources of Conflict Between Sexes"; Science Times of *The New York Times*; P. C14; June 13, 1989.

only doing it your way. As a friend of mine ironically said after coming out of an assertiveness training session, "Gosh, you mean you can be flexible? There isn't only one path to get what you want?" He had finally admitted to himself his propensity to think only in a straight and narrow line, seeing only one answer and not allowing room for other options.

◀ WISDOM: Premarital contracting underscores how each of you are committed to staying together, and that, because of your relationship's importance, both of you are willing to be open.

## Each premarital contracting session has a beginning, a middle, and an end

Your intimate contracting structure has three main parts: the beginning—presentation of your issue; the middle—creatively thinking of alternatives; and the end—choosing the solution that best fulfills your and your partner's needs. Knowing where you are in that process helps you both maintain productive contracting.

## *The beginning of negotiating a premarital contract: Becoming familiar with the issue to be resolved

Before you speak with your partner about what you want to negotiate, prepare your presentation. Phrase your introduction so that your mate does not feel overwhelmed or attacked, but can concentrate on what you are saying. Your goal is to make sure that he understands what you hope to accomplish. Remember that you want to deal with your specific subject, not be diverted by extraneous spin-offs. Also, when your partner initiates a contracting session, listen with compassion, and, when you first respond, phrase your comments positively. You are not catering to your lover by being responsive to his needs.

## *The middle of intimate negotiation: Creative problem solving

A major hurdle has been crossed; you have expressed your concerns and your lover has heard them. But solutions to your problem can still seem unattainable. Most likely, your issue is painful and difficult or it would have been resolved already. While in the beginning stage of negotiation it is imperative to specifically describe your issue, once you and your partner are in dialogue—when you are developing alternatives—it is important that you both remain open to suggestions so that you don't limit your choices. There is no one right answer. The more ideas you come up with to choose from, to expand on, and to compound the more likely you will settle on a joint solution. Think up wild suggestions; premarital contracting discussions need spice as much as sugar to distill their seriousness. Brainstorming is fun; it can lighten the atmosphere and may lead to a solution you would not have thought possible. Jessica explains why she has confidence that her and Marty's negotiations will result in solutions, "We always try to concentrate on our similar wishes, rather than on our differences. That way we tend to come up with ideas that at the very least don't tick one or the other of us off."

## *The end product of negotiation: A constructively developed solution.

Premarital negotiation challenges lovers to separate themselves from their problems. The problem is the issue; not you and your lover. You have already established that you love each other and are committed to one another. Why else would you be contracting?

### What's in it for you and me?

For many people the overriding fear of committing to a relationship is that they don't have a sense of the extent of the partnership boundaries. Premarital contracting presents opportunities for lovers to know what their partners expect in a direct, responsible manner, rather than in philosophical and romantic terms. "Till death us do part," is an old-fashioned promise that we can no longer count on as a fixed guarantee. It is up to us to actively maintain our relationship by communicating clearly to our mates what we want, how we are comfortable, angry, happy, or sad, and come to terms. Premarital contracting expedites lovers' efforts to build a relationship that works.

### Where do we begin talking this time?

The *whys* of your answers make your lover wise!

- Can you and your mate discuss issues even if you have opposite ideas?
- Is your way the only right way?
- Does your partner expect you to take care of him or does he share in the work it takes to have a healthy relationship?
- If your mate is upset, do you feel personally at fault?
- When things don't go the way you would like them to, do you blame your partner, or do you take responsibility for what you want?
- How do you want to communicate with your partner?

### Discussion starter:

- Share a romantic fantasy that you would like to experience with your lover.

For those of you who would like to do some additional reading on the subject of this chapter, the following books are suggested:

*Perfect Women,* Colette Dowling
*The Inner Male: Overcoming Roadblocks To Intimacy,* Herb Goldberg, Ph.D.
*Stage II Relationships: Love Beyond Addiction,* Earnie Larsen
*Toward A New Psychology of Men,* Jean Baker Miller, M.D.
*Toward A New Psychology of Women,* Jean Baker Miller, M.D.

# 5 What's There To Talk About?

*Couples face predictable themes of conflict.*

> How can I know what I think till I see what I say?
>
> W. H. AUDEN

Do you want children if you have to be the primary parent?

Does your career count for more than your mate's?

Will you have the final say since you make the most money?

"WHOSE FAMILY are we going to spend Thanksgiving with?" Stephen asks Jill. This question is the harbinger of many stressful holiday discussions for stepfamilies, as surely as thunder forewarns the coming of a rainstorm. Alternating yearly visits with one another's relatives may be an easy solution for many first-time married couples, but Jill and Stephen, each married for the second time, have a more complicated family tree. Stepchildren from both sides of a remarriage make the parental lineage multiply. "Blended" families must frequently consider non-custodial parents' plans as well as their own. Add to that confusion any children born of the new marriage and it is easy to see that stepfamilies' extended familial obligations would challenge a computer's ability to schedule holiday visits so that no one feels offended. Lovers with children from prior marriages can use premarital contracting to iron out potential wrinkles in their new family structure ahead of time.

### Issues exist, but so do solutions

Studies of premarital and marital couples illustrate that there are general areas of conflict: money, sex, housework, and child care. Today, couples of all ages face similar questions, but with varied permutations and degrees of difficulty. What is painful and distressing for one couple, or one partner, may not faze another. A situation that challenges one couple's creativity to the nth degree might be easy for other partners to resolve.

Lovers can face these common issues or hide from them. The choice is up to you. The goal of this chapter is to stimulate awareness of what your daily issues and general legal stances might be, and to present ideas that may inspire you to positive solutions. The chapters in Part III explain how your solutions can fit into personal covenants and legally binding prenuptial agreements.

### Money issues: Whose money is it? What's mine is mine. What's yours is mine. Or is it ours? Or is it yours?

How to treat our money is one of the most volatile aspects of a relationship. Although financial issues come to the surface in many ways, independence versus dependence is a frequent theme. After all, in our society, money is power.

### *Question #1: What's mine is mine?

A friend's mom talks to us in her New England carriage house. A widow in her sixties, she stands at the stove making coffee for Lynn and me. She keeps right on talking. "Honey," Ruth explains, "your father was very generous to us." Now, recently widowed a second time, she recalls, "When I married your stepfather George, it didn't occur to me to check his attitudes about his money, my money, or our mutual expenses."

Ruth continues, "So frightened that George would spend their inheritance on me, his children, like modern-day Cassandras, warned him of what horrors could happen. Wanting to be a good father, George wouldn't allow himself to be generous to me. He was," she says, shaking her head, "terribly stingy. Instead of discussing his kids' concerns with me, and at least finding out how I felt, George just changed overnight."

Fortunately, Ruth had assets of her own. Although she empathized with George's concerns, she admits, "I was a bit resentful." Now facing a third marriage and disheartened by what she has experienced, she wonders what to do. She tells her daughter to "be careful." But Lynn and I, discussing this conversation on the drive home, think Ruth is warning herself.

A friend in her thirties tells me, "My salary is my security and independence. It gives me the right to speak up in my marriage." She says, "Years ago, I promised myself that I would never stop working." Visiting New York, I listen to a woman on the subway, apparently in her fifties. She confides to her co-straphanger that her salary is "my nest egg. If I go out with the girls and Joe foots my bill, he hassles me. He probably does it to feel that he is in control." Partners, men and women, have to be aware and care how they link themselves with their money.

## *Question #2: What's mine is mine; what's yours is yours?

Is it being selfish to maintain control over your assets, or is it being responsible for yourself? Does it mean you don't trust your partner, or that you choose to actively take care of what is yours? Money and assets are part of one's identity, security, and responsibility. In other words, our financial resources are part and parcel of our sense of autonomy. But marriage does mean commitment, and when you make such a covenant you put restraints on your independence. Successful marriage means thinking of your lover while you determine your actions. It presupposes a commitment to work toward common goals. Marriages require money; but whose and how are decisions for partners to make together. There is no better time to contract about these issues than before you marry.

### *Question #3: What's ours?

M. Dee Samuels says, "It is clear in my law practice that 'Who pays for the living expenses?' questions are the most common ones people try to answer in their day-to-day decisions." Whether you and your mate make a great deal of money, or an average amount, money is an issue that needs attention.

*Two-profession/equal-income household solution.* Rebecca says, "We had no *we* bills until our children arrived. Now, Larry pays the *we* bills for the house that we jointly own and I pay our child care bills." She adds, "I also pay the phone bills since I make most of the long distance calls." Fortunately, contracts and solutions need not be carved in stone. Flexible contracting attitudes lead to flexible solutions as your life together progresses.

*Unequal income, equivalent investment into the "ours" bucket solution.* Attorney Trine Bech describes one couple's arrangement, "They pooled all of their income, even though their financial earning capacity was lopsided. They wanted to go into their marriage as equal economic partners." Another disparate income scenario is one in which the woman has a higher income than her man. Will he feel 'kept,' or will she feel overwhelmed by the financial responsibilities heaped on her shoulders? Finally, a traditional breadwinner/housewife couple, facing the empty-nest syndrome, question whether their past arrangement is one they still want to live under. She feels too dependent and he is tired of being the only one to fulfill their economic needs. They have begun looking at new possibilities.

\* \* \*

Allen and Cindy, an unequal income couple, have worked out a solution that they think is fair. Allen owns a thriving mail order catalog company. Although a survivor of two prior, costly divorces, he has again accrued assets. Cindy and he met at a business convention. She is a successful saleswoman who has already built her nest egg, "I have a sizeable reserve saved so that if anything stops me from working, I could maintain my current lifestyle for at least a year."

Twelve years ago, while their relationship was getting serious, Allen had invited Cindy to work for him. They had, and still have, an honest and forthright work and personal relationship. Now married for ten years, Cindy remembers her reticence when Allen first suggested that they write a prenuptial agreement. She explains, "I went through contracting, though, because of his divorce experiences." They did produce a prenuptial agreement, but Allen just put it in their safe deposit box, unsigned. Cindy says, "Allen told me that going through the contracting process had satisfied his worries. My responses to his concerns encouraged him to have faith in our future ability to work things out whether we stayed married or ended up divorcing."

Cindy and I meet in a pub near her office to discuss her premarital negotiations. Our conversation crosses over the french fries we are devouring. Dressed simply in forest green slacks and a mint colored silk blouse, Cindy carries with her an aura of self-confidence. She explains their financial philosophy, "Our monetary arrangements were simple. This is you and what you are making now, and this is me and what I am making now. We want to get married. We don't want to fight over money in the future! You have your bank account, I have my bank account. Nobody can touch each other's account. We put that in our contract.

"We opened a new joint, savings account and it is a symbol of our partnership. Allen makes far more money than I do, although I make more than enough for me with some left over to help my sister and mom. Recognizing our income differential, Allen bent my way. We each put the same percentage of our income into our joint bank account, but Allen puts in more cash than I do. If we ever get divorced, we agreed that we'll split whatever cash is in our joint bank account down the middle. The rest of our separate incomes go into our personal accounts. We established what each of us contributes for rent, food, and other living expenses in proportion to our incomes, responsibilities, and chores."

Whether a couple consists of dual-career partners, traditional breadwinner/housewife split, househusband and breadwinner, or student and income producer, there are money issues to discuss. Living expenses need to be paid, savings to plan for, and future goals to be considered. How each of you want to treat your money can have vast relationship consequences that will seek you out whether or not you attend to them through premarital contracting.

### *"What ifs!"*

There are so many "what ifs" in life that it is impossible to prepare ourselves for each and every potentiality. But we can have our eyes open, and there are certain categories that are "for sures." Health, life, and disability insurance, for example, are important to plan for. Allen and Cindy took care of life insurance arrangements in their same fair manner. Cindy's invalid sister is her beneficiary. Allen's policy names his two sons as beneficiaries of one half and Cindy receives the other half. Both of them pay the premiums on the policies with the same percentage arrangement as for their savings.

### *How do we want to live?*

Lifestyle issues become "what if" questions that challenge premarital couples to talk ahead of time. Certain aspects of lifestyle concerns can be put in prenuptial agreements, others benefit from clarification but don't need the support of the law. In either case, intimate contracting gives you the dynamics to be responsible for your issues in caring ways.

## *Lifestyle issues: Work plans and dreams*

Couples who engage in the premarital contracting process to define their career goals can raise a number of questions to think and talk about. Although some of your plans are not immediately applicable, they may be relevant to your joint future.

### *Question #1: Whose job takes precedence, yours or mine?

Both men and women are striving to be successful in their careers. No longer does the man's job take priority over the woman's— without each partner agreeing to that preference in one way or another. Whereas in the past relocation decisions did not raise the question of whether to move, but only whether it was a beneficial step for his career, now, if both partners work, they have two careers to consider.

Heidi and Joel came to that crossroads prepared ahead of time by their premarital negotiations. They had their career-decision-making rule ready: when a choice had to be made that would affect them both, they agreed to alternate who made the selection. Generally the influencing factor on the decision maker was the place each of them was at in their careers. Another process utilized by a corporate couple facing possible relocation was "whoever did not have the offer made the basic decision to move."[1] It is easier to have your system worked out before the fact rather than having to react when the circumstances are forcing you to the wall. By negotiating your possible alternatives during your premarital preparation, you save on stress later.

---

1. Rosanna Hertz; *More Equal Than Others: Women and Men in Dual-Career Marriages*; University of California Press; Berkeley; 1986; p. 57.

## *Question #2: Which comes first, the office or us?

Time together versus time spent at the office is a dilemma many lovers face. Change the word "office" to any other obligation you have and you and your mate may be faced with yet other diametrically opposing pulls. As love-partners, we have committed ourselves because we want to spend our lives together, haven't we? Togetherness can mean different things to each of you.

> Tony and Nancy are very much in love, but they have a problem that brings conflict to their long relationship. Tony is a fledgling stockbroker. He puts in long hours making phone calls and running seminars to drum up new clients. Nancy is more settled in her job and her hours are more regular. She has begun to resent Tony's time away from "us." Tony, exasperated, explains, "But this is the most important time in my career. These are the years I have to push to succeed. Five years more and then I can relax."

If both partners need room to work on their careers, they will be sympathetic to each other's situation. But if one is going full-speed ahead, and the other is not progressing at his job, or has less pressure to produce, new issues of time allocation will surface. Use your premarital contracting to clarify your personal expectations.

## *Question #3: What do I want to do now?

Career options and goals of one partner will color the whole partnership. Both lovers need to share their thoughts and hear their mate's input. Perhaps one partner hopes to make a career change. Loss of that person's salary, expenses due to tuition, or the strain of extra hours studying away from home may be in the offing. Maybe your spouse isn't interested in working hard, but only willing to make enough money to pay for some extras; is that in alignment with your expectations? To create your solutions, each of you has to be actively involved in your premarital contracting.

## *Lifestyle issues: The blessed event; or is it?*

Supercouples, both in high-wire careers, can support one another at times of stress just by being familiar with what they both are going through. In *More Equal Than Others*, Professor Hertz points out that not through liberated gender philosophy, but because of career pressures, these couples have equalized their roles and responsibilities. However, once a child arrives, everything takes on a different dimension. Responsibility for your children is a constant. Your toddlers cannot be shoved in a corner if the baby-sitter doesn't come or if they are too sick to go to child care.

## *Question #1: Are you Superwoman/Superman?

Although you may know the cost of wanting to do it all, you still might be tempted to try. But too much on one set of shoulders strains more than muscles. Couples with "S" on their capes can support themselves by reviewing what they are trying to accomplish.

There are alternatives to doing it all. One possibility that has been covered frequently in the media is the "mommy track." Mommy trackers are women who choose to get off the high speed career route so that they can spend more time with their young children. The cost to them, though, is less chance of a promotion or a partnership. A silent question that haunts corporate hallowed halls is—where is the "daddy track"? Another solution to work overload is a phenomenon aptly titled "sequencing." Mostly women, but some men as well, work full time until they have children. Then, they shift their work load to accommodate their primary child caretaking responsibilities. Once the children are in school, sequencers go back to work part time. Full-time work begins again once the children are older.

For many premarital couples who, marrying later in life, plan to have children quickly, the issue is how to be career persons, lovers, and parents at the same time? In the sixties movie *The Graduate* plastics was the secret word; for the lovers of the nineties, logistics is. Some child-raising options for new parents are to give up your career; have part-time or full-time third party child care; work at home; or any combination of the above. Each possibility brings forth questions to look at with your partner because they will affect the structure of your relationship.

Some premarital child-care topics that can have long-term consequences are: if you leave your career for an extended period, can you return to the level you left? If you stay at your job, which of you will stay home when your child is sick? If you do choose your child as your top priority, will that influence your job rating? Can you expect to have any time, energy, or desire left for quality time with your children if you are working full time or part time?

> Fran, a civil engineer I met, describes what she and many other women face in Superwoman mode, "I'm really pulled in many different directions. Do you want to hear an example that really tells it all? I took time off to go on my son's class trip, but when I wanted to go to the office Saturday to make up for not working the day of Danny's trip my husband was insulted that I would leave him on the weekend. I want to be a caring wife, so I stayed home. It's hard to do and be everything; sometimes it's almost too much."

## *Question #2: Whose baby is it?

In *More Equal Than Others* the author observes corporate dual-career couples, "Remarkably, their discussions all come to the same conclusion: it is the wife who should decide to have or not to have children, as she is the one who has the most to lose in the workplace."[2] The assumption that the child is the wife's responsibility holds true for other couples too. Studies show that women still do most of the work at home, and in fact, "They worked an *extra month of twenty-four-hour days a year.*"[3] The second shift is an alternative, but

---

2. Hertz; *More Equal Than Others*; p. 136.
3. Arlie Hochschild with Anne Machung; *Second Shift: Working Parents and the Revolution At Home*; Viking Penguin, Inc.; New York; 1989; p. 3. Italics are Ms. Hochschild's.

destructive resentments invade partnerships that sanction uneven contributions.

Just as two incomes have become more of a necessity for a couple's survival, so too must partners, to keep their marriage healthy, accept joint responsibility for family matters. Your premarital negotiations needn't be chiseled in stone, but discussing options can help you plan.

## *Question #3: Where is my office; what is my job?

Do men really have the freedom to be "househusbands"? In my travels around the country, I have spoken with couples in which the man is the primary homemaker and/or parent. It is still rare, and the attitudes of those around them range from not noticing anything unusual to total disgust—which I interpret to be confusion. Why would a man wander down such a path rather than have his wife walk it?

There are couples in which the husband can more likely work at home than the wife. Other reasons exist as well for men to choose to be househusbands: perhaps the man's wife makes a higher income and has better company benefits, or he wants to be the primary parent and she doesn't. Whether full-time or part-time parents, men, by being actively involved with their families, are experiencing the emotional awareness and parental joy that has previously been reserved for women.

Be flexible, creative, and always loving to yourself as well as to your mate when you consider family lifestyle issues. Some questions lovers may want to consider are: which of us will take a leave of absence or make a career change? Who could work at home or will commit to being the primary parent? The answers to these questions are decisions to make and remake as you and your partner's options rearrange themselves. Premarital contracting skills become marital skills that will support you as you meet life's challenges.

## *Question #4: Stepping out with my baby, and yours, and ours. How can we blend our families?

The simple, clear-cut, traditional family structure has been stretched out of shape by the proliferation of divorce and remarriage. The Census Bureau estimated that in 1987 there were 4.3 million step-families with 8.7 million minor children in the United States.[4] Lovers who are parents already and are considering joining their families can be overly sensitive to how their partners relate with their children. Are they friendly enough, or do they expect too much?

We also may wonder if we can love our mate's children, or if we have to love them. Overwhelmed with responsibilities for our own youngsters, will we have enough resilience to relate to stepchildren? Once your relationship progresses, more concrete questions will form for you and your partner to discuss in your premarital contracting. As well, there are pertinent questions to ask yourself. Am I too critical of his children? Do I expect too much of her kids? Who has priority? Partners will have to support each other when "wicked stepparent" reactions surface. It is a powerful archetype that intrudes into many blended families; one that is hard not to take personally.

Premarital contracting can help you and your mate set up guidelines before emotional confrontations sap the energy of your relationship. Stepfamilies facing the unknown can make new traditions and rules. New stepparents Jay and Christine explain, "We settled on some house rules, but gave the kids time to get used to them, keeping in mind that they were in shock, just like us." Friends of mine, who, once their forces were joined, were proud parents/stepparents of five children, worked hard to get their two groups melded into a functional family. One of the first items on their agenda was creating joint traditions that were new for everybody. It isn't easy to join a ready-made family with traditions, roles, and hierarchy already established.

There are also newly blended families, like Bob's and mine, in which the stepchildren are teenagers and older. Mature offspring have a philosophical awareness that can support the new family, but they

---

4. Lawrence Kutner; "In Blended Families, Rivalries Intensify"; *The New York Times*, Parent & Child Section; January 5, 1989; p. C1

too have their resentments. One lady in her sixties, sitting next to me on a plane trip to Seattle, remembers when her eighty-year-old father had told her he was marrying a dear friend, "I had to laugh at myself. I could see how happy he was and my mother has been gone for the past ten years, but it was still hard for me to welcome this new woman in her place." Will our children ever relinquish the glorified picture of their parents together, no matter what the reality?

## *Question #5: Do you want to have children?

Now more than ever, it is an option, not an expectation, for partners to become parents. This decision has many factors to consider other than fulfillment of grandparental dreams, or touted primal urges. Yes, a child of your own offers opportunity for incredible love and fulfillment. But children reach into your pocketbook and may limit your career goals.

My teenage daughter and her girlfriends were very supportive and happy for me while Bob and I went through our courtship. ARP, and into our marriage. Very interested in my premarital contracting process, the girls and I had many lengthy conversations about expectations of job and marriage. They all knew they wanted to work, and they wanted to marry and have a family. But when we wondered how to juggle career, marriage, and children, no one had even a fantasy to present. "Oh sure," I said to myself, "they're only teenagers, still young. Wait." Now in college, more seriously thinking about their future—they still don't have a clear idea. They are sure though, that they want to do it all.

My daughter and her friends do not have unique dreams. "Last year, two-thirds of married women 20 to 34 years old were working, according to the United States Department of Labor, and a Census Bureau Survey indicated that almost nine-tenths of all working women in that age bracket expected to become pregnant."[5] Whether couples are in their twenties, thirties, or forties, and although they

---

5. Sara Rimer; "Women, Jobs, and Children: A New Generation Worries"; *The New York Times*; Sunday, November 27, 1988; p. 1.

may have waited until they are secure in their careers, financially comfortable, and set in their marriages, child-rearing stress and strain cannot be avoided. All the more reason loving couples ought to engage in premarital contracting so that they can prepare themselves for the future.

## *Lifestyle issues never cease: Family planning*

### *Income needs:

If you commit to being a full-time parent, how does that change your income and lifestyle? Is that okay with the two of you? If your mate raises your children and you earn the money, are you equal partners?

### *Religion; a personal choice:

Once the children arrive and it is time to think of the moral values you want to instill, there are more issues to examine together. If you are an interfaith couple, whose religion will your family follow, or will you incorporate two traditions? How will you tell your parents? These questions require far-reaching answers. Premarital contracting helps keep the search on track.

### *Your surname Sir:

Which last name will your children carry? Hyphenated surnames, once a sign of upper crust lineage, now announce a couple's recognition of her last name as well as his. One set of premarital partners decided to keep their own surnames, but they had a creative arrangement. In their premarital contract, they agreed that their children's surnames would be the last name of the parent of the opposite sex. Years passed after their first child was born, however, and they could not have a second child. This couple amended their prenuptial agreement and added the second parent's surname to their child's last name.

## More "What ifs"

What if your parents became incapacitated, or what if there is a shift in a blended family's child custody responsibilities? Finally, the big "WHAT IFs": Divorce and Death. Why must "what ifs" be so catastrophic? How about, what if one of us wins the lottery?

## Disaster issues: Widowhood and divorce

Lovers ask themselves, "How can I bring up the possibility of us divorcing? It will seem like I don't have confidence in our love." But statistics tell us divorce can happen, even as our hearts declare that it couldn't. It is "what if" time again. The subjects that you have to think about in case of divorce are issues that also could cause pain if one of you dies or becomes incapacitated. Establishing child support or asset distribution in case of divorce, incapacity, or death builds mutual trust. More practically, discussing preventive measures will help you plan how you want to handle such issues in general. Disaster concerns can usually be alleviated by prenuptial agreements in conjunction with wills.

## *Question #1: In case of disaster, why think of our children?

Your children are your responsibility and must be protected in the following ways: emotionally, because they are yours; practically, because children cannot survive on their own; and legally, because if not taken care of they might become a burden on the state. Your children's future is your responsibility. Sadly, the reality is, "Most divorced men provide surprisingly little financial support for their children. According to the Bureau of the Census in 1985, 81 percent of divorced fathers and 66 percent of separated fathers have court orders to pay child support. Twenty percent of these fathers fully comply with the court order; 15 percent pay irregularly. (And how much child support a father pays is not related to his capacity to pay.)"[6] Contracting while you are in the embrace of romantic love engenders reasonable evenhanded settlements should they become necessary later. Think of just-in-case-of-divorce scenarios in which you could stay connected with your kids. One covenant might be to agree to joint time and effort custody. Additionally, there are concrete actions, such as making wills and taking out life insurance, that you can take to protect your children in case one or both of you die.

Discussing child care and support is an opportunity for both lovers to show commitment to their planned for children, whether they stay together or separate due to divorce or widowhood. Sharing thoughts about how you want your family to interact can be a wonder filled time for premarital contractors. Your love for each other will be strengthened as you see how both of you care.

### *Question #2: In case of disaster, why think of my spouse?

Male or female, you may decide to give up your income producing work to take care of your children, or you might choose to support your spouse's career move which in turn could limit your job opportunities. You may contract to finance your spouse while he gets additional, professional training. Unfortunately, as Lenore Weitzman notes in her book *The Divorce Revolution*, after the first year following their divorce, on average, women have a 73 percent loss in their standard of living, while men at the same time carry a 42 percent gain. How do you want to protect yourself and your mate in case your partnership doesn't pan out? Do you expect recognition for the sacrifices you may incur, such as career path closing down, salary loss, or money spent? The court may not show appreciation for your supportive actions on behalf of your mate and family, but you can give

---

6. Hochschild; *The Second Shift*; p. 249

it to each other ahead of time in your premarital contracting solutions.

## Personal lifestyle issues

Lovers talking about personal issues not only clear the air but they also develop a pattern for solving future conflicts.

## *Issue #1: Personal habits

Leaving underwear on the floor, stockings hanging all over the bathroom, and being too neat or too messy are little things that can become big annoyances as intimate relationships progress. If you promise yourself that you will get him to change once you marry, or that you will ask her to transform herself once the wedding bonds have been tied, forget it, it won't happen. The saying, "Your right to swing your fist ends where my nose begins" is a two-sided message. One side warns lovers that it is futile to count on changing your partner. But the flip side says that you can let your partner know where your space is and how far he can enter without intruding. Through constructive premarital contracting, lovers can modify themselves as they learn their partner's values.

## *Issue #2: The hidden plum

Sexual expectations, fears, and desires are issues whether we talk about them openly or not. How do you feel about fidelity? One husband, chuckling, told me, "Since it would bother her if I were unfaithful but I maintained it wouldn't bother me if she were, we posed this arrangement. She could be unfaithful, but I wouldn't. After we laughed, we both pledged to a monogamous relationship. Neither of us wanted the intrusion of mistrust into our intimacy." Sex and love are intricately connected in personal relationships, woven together by trust. It is here partners are excruciatingly vulnerable. Trust between lovers may be given rashly, but for trust to remain, it must be carefully treated.

You can be assured of your mate's love in positive ways. A touch of her hand on your shoulder or his holding your hand can express your feelings for each other. We do need verification that we are loved. Does your mate show enough affection for you? Can you talk to your lover about how you want to make love? The pressure put on men to initiate lovemaking may be as burdensome and as restrictive as waiting is for women. Both of you have ideas and fantasies to pursue. As with other premarital contracting, each of you can participate in your lovemaking as you choose to.

### Intimate contracting: Control or commitment

Brooke and Sean plan to marry. After receiving her MBA, Brooke became an efficiency expert for a management consulting firm. She is used to people acting on her advice. Sean runs a large hardware store. He enjoys Brooke's self-assuredness, but lately they have been having frequent arguments. Brooke has become very bossy. Sean, who respects her opinions, nonetheless, has his own too and doesn't always want to do things her way. Sean says, "I finally told her that she was acting like a dictator." Brooke explains, "Sometimes I forget that although my business is problem solving, Sean is an expert in our relationship too." Sean and Brooke are learning to merge each other's advice into joint solutions rather than battling for whose ideas should be followed.

### Premarital covenants

Your prenuptial agreement may be written on a piece of stationery, it may be a legal document prepared by lawyers, or simply a list you and your mate verbally agreed to. Whichever form your love-covenant takes it confirms what you two hope to live by. Many couples choose to go through the contracting process, and some of them prepare a prenuptial agreement. Other couples don't see the need to sign a contract once they have negotiated through their options and straightened out their issues. Bob and I did execute our premarital agreement so that it would be a lawfully binding contract. But before we did, we extracted from our legal document most of our lifestyle declarations and incorporated them into our private covenant. Although those pledges could not be enforced by law, we knew we would follow them.

## What's there to talk about?

Attorney Trine Bech says, "The best thing about private contracting is that it puts issues on the table." Intimate contracting doesn't end with the resolution of a particular issue. There are always new ramifications to life's conditions. The good news is that whatever issue appears, as you and your mate gain in premarital contracting skill, you will have the ability to talk things through and form a joint settlement. Although coming to mutually agreeable solutions is challenging, it can be done.

### Where do we begin talking this time?
Your *whys* make your lover wise.
"What ifs":

- What if you want to go back to school?
- What if your mate chooses to relocate?
- What if your partner wants to keep her assets separate from yours?
- What if you want to have a family?
- What if your mate has children from a prior marriage?
- What if you want to have a prenuptial agreement?

### Discussion starter:

- Talk about particularly wonderful ways your lover supports you when you are upset.

*Some sources for support in clarifying your issues:*

**PREPARE-ENRICH:** David H. Olson, Ph.D., Professor and Director of Graduate Studies, Department of Family Social Science of the University of Minnesota, is President of Prepare-Enrich, Inc. He and his associates have developed series of questions for premarrieds ("Prepare"—for unmarried couples without children—and "Prepare MC"—for unmarried couples with children) that, once answered, are interpreted under counselors' supervision, "to help learn more about *yourself, your partner,* and *your relationship.*" For more information contact:

> PREPARE-ENRICH, Inc.
> P. O. Box 190
> Minneapolis, MN 55458-0190
> 1-800-331-1661

Stepfamily Association of America, 602 Joppa Road, Baltimore, MD 21204.

Stepfamily Foundation, 333 West End Avenue, New York, NY 10023.

New Ways to Work, 149 Ninth Street, San Francisco, CA 94103.

For those of you who would like to do some additional reading on the subject of this chapter:

"Contractual Ordering Of Marriage: A New Model For State Policy," *California Law Review,* March 1982, Marjorie Maguire Shultz

*Funny Sauce,* Dehlia Ephron (Stepfamilies)

*Justice, Gender, and the Family,* Susan Moller Okin

*More Equal Than Others: Women and Men in Dual-Career Marriages,* Rosanna Hertz

"The Baby Boom"; *The New York Times,* "The Good Health Magazine," October 8, 1989, Carin Rubenstein

*The Divorce Revolution: The Unexpected Social And Economic Consequences For Women And Children In America,* Lenore Weitzman

*The Marriage Contract: Spouses, Lovers, and the Law,* Lenore Weitzman

*The Nurturing Father,* Kyle Pruett

*The Second Shift: Working Parents and the Revolution At Home,* Arlie
Hochschild with Anne Machung

*The Sexual Politics Of Housework,* "Utne Reader," March/April 1990

*Yours, Mine and Ours,* Dr. Anne C. Bernstein

*Women and Home-Based Work: The Unspoken Contract,* Kathleen
Christensen

# III

## THE PREMARITAL CONTRACTING PROCESS

Lovers who know their goals can use covenants, Contract Law, and experts as resources; partners who contract will save their marriage ahead of time.

# 6 In This Troth Do We Pledge?

*You can develop your own marriage covenant.*

> The mark of a healthy relationship is not the absence of conflict, but its effective management and resolution. [1]
>
> MARJORIE MAGUIRE SHULTZ, J.D.

Do you trust your mate?

Do you think that stating what you want in your marriage means fighting with your lover?

Do you feel as morally committed to the pledges you make to your partner as you do to the ones you promise in business situations?

"IF YOU HAVE to make a prenuptial agreement, you shouldn't get married!" My son wasn't the only one to proclaim such doubts. Friends and relatives responded with misgivings when the fact that Bob and I were writing a prenuptial agreement came up in conversation. Face-to-face with the premarital contract's loathsome image, I would explain, "We are using our premarital contracting to clear up issues that are important to us before we marry. This way, we have

---

1. Marjorie Maguire Shultz; "Contractual Ordering Of Marriage: A New Model For State Policy"; *California Law Review*; Volume 70, No. 2; March 1982; p. 308.

taken care of our concerns ahead of time. We want to make sure our marriage lasts." Silent responses; heads shake, "Yes, it makes sense"; mouths smile, "Oh I see, you do love each other."

## How can premarital contracting work for you?

We have the right to orchestrate our marital partnership. But there is no one correct path to success, so we lovers must create our guidelines. Constructive premarital contracting gives you and your mate the support to define your marriage. To help you determine what you want from your premarital covenants, ask yourself why you are contracting. Your partner's answers, combined with yours, can become the philosophical core of your premarital covenants. The primary reason that motivated Bob and me through the labyrinthine passages of our contracting was that we wanted to optimize our ability to stay together for the rest of our lives while protecting our interests in case we separate.

### *Tie the knot

Allen and Cindy, contractors in the chapter "What's There To Talk About?", exemplify how premarital lovers' joint outlook can become their contracting motivation. Allen says, "When we began to put together our prenuptial agreement, the discussions were abrasive to Cindy because she felt that they presumed the removal of the 'forever and ever' of our marriage even before we tied the knot."

Cindy explains why she did contract despite her misgivings, "I agreed to negotiate with Allen because of the failures of his past two marriages, but I wasn't happy about it." Allen, who was forty-three and the father of two sons, bore deep scars from his divorces. He wanted to have a loving relationship, but educated by his life experience he was looking for assurances before Cindy and he were married. Cindy understood why Allen wanted a contract, but her attitude was and still is: "Personally, I don't feel the need for one. I can take care of myself. I know if I fall, I'll jump back on my feet. God knows, I've done it before."

Had Cindy refused to participate, or simply not taken care of herself in their contracting discussions, most likely, Allen's uneasiness would have increased. Instead, Cindy's belief in herself made their contracting sessions productive, and reassured Allen. Cindy went into the process wholeheartedly. "I decided if I was going to do this thing for Allen, I also would do it for myself. There wasn't much that I needed, but I knew what I did want and I went for it. Allen was also clear about the conditions he wanted." Their philosophical credo: we will each take care of our own needs, but always be fair to one another.

## *Badge of courage*

We know that "stand up and fight" is a call for a clear type of courage. The enemy is identified, the wrong is defined, and the battle lines are drawn. Premarital contracting is not a war between enemies, but caring communication between lovers. It does not have to be adversarial; yet, fear of possible friction keeps many intimate partners from contracting. You are not declaring war when you let your mate know what you want to happen in your relationship. But you do need special courage and resolution to speak up for yourself and also, to hear what your partner wants. Premarital contracting takes tremendous bravery. Acknowledging that not contracting leads lovers into traps sparks lovers' courage.

## *Trap: If you don't contract, you can never know for sure who your partner is

If lovers assume who and what their mate will be—instead of telling one another what is—they will end up dissatisfied. Misled by their assumptions, they are not prepared when reality strikes unexpectedly.

Susan is a talented, freelance costume designer. She towers over me as we walk, chatting and sipping our wine. Slowly passing by the different pieces of art at a gallery opening in Soho, we listen to her new husband Jim's jazz trio play. Not yet flush with money, Susan and Jim can't parcel their home responsibilities out to third parties. Before they married and moved in together, she had assumed that they would both be responsible for cleaning their apartment. Sue tells me, "We never really spoke about who would do what. I just figured since he was so supportive of my work, he would pitch in when we were home."

Surprisingly, that notion hadn't entered Jim's mind. When Jim and I talk later, he explains, "My mom takes care of everything at home. I never learned how. Anyway, things are pretty clean, it's only the two of us." Jim and Susan have expectations that, if not attended to, will lead to disappointment.

◀ Premarital contracting herds assumptions out into the open where they can be lassoed, branded, and dispersed in appropriate directions.

## *Trap: If you don't nourish your love, it can't grow

Premarital contracting supports lovers trying to solve daily conflicts and major policy issues. Its structure connects you and your mate. You each speak out about your values, thus acknowledging yourselves; and you both listen, thus recognizing each other.

◀ Premarital contracting partners nurture their love by responding caringly to each other.

### *What do you mean, a covenant?*

A covenant, pledge, or vow (words embedded in love and marriage) between two lovers who are promising one another what they will or will not be, do or not do, is a premarital agreement. Whatever form of covenant a couple chooses, it is an explicit pact between them, reached through a communication process that includes revelation, decision making, and resolution. Each partner chooses whether their part in the process will be active or reactive. Both of you can use premarital contracting for your individual and your mutual benefit. You are not contracting because you do not trust each other, but because you do trust in each other's commitment. With no assumptions or hidden messages, premarital contracting allows you to work out what you both agree to stand by.

## *Intimate contracting is not so unusual

Wills are personal pledges that clearly define what we want to happen once we die. They are intimate commitments to people we love. Certainly, they express current feelings and goals. As well, we check with attorneys to ensure that the will is legally correct. It is also all right to contract with your lover about what you want to happen during your life.

*Whether your agreements are verbal, written on a matchbook cover, or signed and sealed legal documents, they are all premarital covenants*

There are four types of premarital covenants: personal verbal promises; private written contracts; public lawful agreements; and unspoken pacts.

## *Verbal covenant:

Charlie and Judyth have been married for many years. Pioneers, they began their premarital contracting during the sixties when both were establishing their careers. Although culturally there were looser gender expectations during those years, there were no new rules, traditions, or customs ready-made for Judyth and Charles to use as guides. So they created their own structure, vowing to have an equal marriage. This verbal covenant was cemented with a pledge, also verbal, to meet every two weeks to talk about how they were adhering to their covenant of equality.

## *Written covenant:

"While we acknowledge our mutual affection by publicly assuming the relationship of husband and wife . . . we deem it a duty to declare that this act on our part implies no sanction of, nor promise of voluntary obedience to such of the present laws of marriage as refuse to recognize the wife as an independent, rational being, while they confer upon the husband an injurious and unnatural superiority."[2]

This contract was written by Lucy Stone and Henry Blackwell in 1855. Fortunately, Family Law has changed and our premarital contracts begin at a better place, but Stone and Blackwell's pledge is relevant, nonetheless.

## *Legal covenant:

When you want a document that lawfully binds you and your mate to what you agree to, you must enter into a proper, formal, legal contract. The chapter "But Why A Legal Contract?" elucidates reasons for a lawful covenant. The chapters "What Makes A Contract A Contract?" and "Your Premarital Agreement" are devoted to the composition of a legal prenuptial agreement. This chapter will help you decide the types of covenants you want to pledge.

## *Unspoken pacts

An unspoken pact is what you enter into if you do or say nothing. If you hate doing the dishes, but find yourself doing them without speaking up to resolve the situation, you have contracted to do the

---

2. Eleanor Flexner; *Century Of Struggle: The Women's Rights Movement In The United States*; Cambridge, Mass.; 1959; p. 64. Quoted in *The Feminine Mystique* by Betty Friedan; A Laurel Book, Dell Publishing Co., Inc.; 1983; p. 90.

dishes. Unspoken pacts bind lovers just as strongly as any up-front premarital contracts will.

## The road to success

Successful premarital contracting requires the synergism of two worlds to work effectively: the public world of careful planning and goal orientation with the private world of emotions and nurturing. Most men have been groomed to operate in some sort of public arena whereas most women have been raised to perform in a personal environment. From the public world we learn to tighten our focus so that we can be successful contractors and create solutions that will achieve our ends. In the personal world we learn to guide our perspectives so that we see more than our own needs; thus we can be cooperative and supportive. Love joins these two worlds.

## Your issues will guide your selection of covenants

Your goals will direct you to the most appropriate covenants. Do you see premarital contracting as a ritual announcing your commitment, as a source of protection for the unknown future, or as a statement that embraces your partnership? There are steps that you can take to help you frame your covenants.

### *First step to select your covenants: Lists and lists—yours and your partner's

Premarital contracting is a process for two lovers, but there are steps we must take as individuals. You and you alone know what you want in your marriage. With paper and pen and an active dialogue between you and yourself, you can capture your concerns, look at them, and decide whether they are worth pursuing further. The lists you and your partner write separately will be combined later to bring your interests together. For now, you can be brief. Bring up anything that crosses your mind. Your lists do not have to consist only of things to worry about. What marvelous ideas do you have that will make your life with your lover soar to the heights of joy? This is not a gloomy time, but one of exploration. To get both of you started on your lists, it may be helpful to set up a time to go over your notes together.

### *Second step to select your covenants: The unveiling— compile your pre-premarital contract lists.

This stage can be a love-filled yet harrowing period. Yes, during your ARP you have shared your dreams, visions, worries, concerns, plans, ambitions, hopes, and fantasies. But now you are doing it for real. What you say is important and will be counted. Yet it can be a phase filled with new awareness of who you both are and how much you love one another. It is a time of listening and sharing. Where do your lists match? How exciting. Where do you lists veer apart? How expanding. Where do your lists lock horns? How scary. When you both are ready, combine your lists. All sorts of interesting topics can be raised.

***Bob and Jacqueline's first joint, pre-prenupital agreement list:*** Our guiding principle: We will respect each other's autonomy

Items to cover

   *Stay together issues
     House
       value as of 10/86
       proceeds from sale when we move
         portion to be used for next house
         portion to be used for nest egg for us
     Undeveloped property in California
       value as of 8/27/87
       proceeds from sale
         portion to be used for next house
         portion to be used for nest egg for us

Our savings:
    not equal in dollar amount
Our salaries:
    not equal in dollar amount
Money to be set aside for Jacqueline's three
children and Bob's daughter
Use of our incomes
    we both want bills paid off immediately,
    we do not want debts
  *If we separate issues
Proceeds from sale of house
Proceeds from sale of land

The purpose of your joint list is to help you open your communication gates and get the two of you talking to each other about your personal subjects. It isn't easy to start, so begin anywhere that calls to you. As has been suggested at the end of earlier chapters, begin your discussions with topics that you enjoy.

## *Third step to select your covenants: More lists

Once you have committed to your first joint list, widen your focus. Think about what your general and specific goals are. Allow your personal attitudes to determine how you look at the categories for discussion. You and your partner can make clear to each other what you are trying to protect, gain, ensure, and avoid for your relationship.

*Jacqueline and Bob's second joint, pre-prenuptial agreement lists:*

Purpose of agreement:
    We want to optimize our ability to stay together for the rest of our lives, while protecting our interests in case we separate. We promise to respect each other's autonomy.

Categories:

Who we are; our separate important life experiences and lessons
  Jacqueline
  Robert

What we bring with us:
  Assets
    Jacqueline
    Robert
  Liabilities
    Jacqueline
    Robert

What we want to keep separate:
  Property
    Jacqueline
    Robert
  Children
  Dog

What we want to share; how we will live together:
  Marital property
  Finances
  Location of marital home
  Careers/sources of income
  Travel

What happens when one or both of us die:
  Testamentary provisions
  Estate rights

If one or both of us want to end the marriage; cooperation:
  Distribution of marital property
  Valuation of assets: date and method
  Maintenance/support
  Debt

*Your categories will determine the shape of your covenants*

The topics that stay on your lists will guide you to the types of covenants that are best for you: verbal pledges, written declarations for
you and your lover's eyes only, or legal contracts. One or all are available to give you comfort. What kind of contracts do your categories
lead you to use?

## *Choice: Personal verbal promises

There are many pledges we make to our mates while in the mists
of our ARP that become part of our relationship. There are certain
vows, however, that stand out as standard bearers for our actions.

> Bev has two children from her first marriage and Steve has three
> from his, two of whom now live with them. Together, they have
> a three-year-old daughter. Married now for the past seven years,
> they reveal to me their code of honor and behavior for their
> "blended" family. As a guest at their Sunday morning breakfast,
> I watch five of their children sitting (not quietly) at the table relat-
> ing easily with each other.
>     The kids know their places in the family structure. All have
> equal importance; none are favored. Essential to Steve's and Bev's
> verbal premarital contract is the first commitment they thought
> of, "Our top priority was knitting our families together." Steve
> continues, "We agreed that the way we would do that was to not
> take sides against each other in conflicts with any of our kids.
> We never let them come between us." This verbal commitment
> remains in force due to Steve and Bev's heroic efforts. Just ask
> any stepparents you know and they will vouch for how difficult
> it is to be the "wicked one."
>     Verbal commitments work. As with any promise lovers
> pledge, the fulfillment comes by being careful about what we
> agree to, remembering our commitments, and doing what we said
> we would do. Bev says, "By discussing our lists, I saw how Steve
> felt about issues, and if anything bothered me I said so. We got

to understand how we each looked at our facts and figures, how we felt about one another and respected each other. That all showed in our decisions."

## *Choice: Private, written contracts

Some of our pledges move us to preserve them in writing. Certain promises bring-joy and we want to relish them, returning to them again and again at celebrations. Other vows that give us peace of mind may need the power of the written word to solidify their existence. Generally, promises about how partners want their lives to flow together fit into this category. They are private decisions that are very important to lovers. The force behind these vows is the moral power of each partner. Bill and Cara, baby Josh's co-parents whom we met in the chapter "Isn't It Romantic?", decided to live together before they married. The following agreement became their premarital covenant:

PROPOSED GUIDELINES FOR LIVING TOGETHER

**Style:** We will try to accept each other's style and rhythm; but, if things become uncomfortable for either one of us, we will express our needs directly and work on a solution together.

**Boxes:** Each of us will have our boxes put away or stored out of sight two weeks after we move in together.

**Cleaning Person:** We will hire a cleaning person to come once a month to do major cleaning. In between the cleaning person's visits, Cara will look to see what major things need to be done and will take care of them to her satisfaction. Bill agrees to participate.

**Bills:** The following scheme indicates who is responsible for making sure mutual bills are paid:

Bill: Electric, City Services, Rent

Cara: Gas, Phone, Garbage, Cleaning Person

**Rooms:** Cara's office will be upstairs. It is to be used and decorated as she wishes. Her office will also serve as a guest room.

Bill will have the major use of their bedroom as far as decorating and usage—except as a shared sleeping area.

**Cooking:** Breakfast and lunches will be on our own unless together by invitation. Dinners will be separate unless planned ahead or by invitation. This is subject to change as we get used to living together.

**Yard work:** We will share the yard work.

**Property:** Personal belongings brought to the household will remain the property of the original owners.

**Mess/Clutter:** Day-to-day cleaning will be the responsibility of the person who made the mess.

**Love:** Each of us is to try to remember that we are living together because we *want* to and because we *love* each other.

**As Individuals:** We each promise to respect the other person and the other individual's Spirit, being mindful that we love each other *because* of the unique differences that make us who we are.

**Growth:** Furthermore, we need to be mindful of our own and the other's personal growth, lending support and being helpful as needed.

**Toilet Paper:** When replacing a roll of toilet paper, it should be placed so that the new sheets come over the top toward the user (as opposed to falling right up next to the wall).

Bill explains his satisfaction with their private written vow, "I didn't feel we needed a legal contract. If we have an agreement about how we would treat certain issues should something come up in the future, I can be held pretty closely to them. I feel that way about Cara too, and she has trust in me."

## *Choice: Public lawful agreements

There are some of our promises that, either because of our personal needs or our home state's Family Law regulations, require the backing of a lawful contract to ensure their preservation. For example, partners who want to establish specific asset arrangements for each other in their estate plans that go beyond their state's rules will need a legal contract to protect their goals. Also, personal divorce experiences that have burned a hole in one's security blanket may be enough motivation to complete a legal contract. I was certainly scarred by my divorce, and I could not agree to marry again without the support and assurance of a legal document to preserve my assets for my children.

*The reinforcement troops are here.* I used the legal power of Bob's and my intended prenuptial agreement to strengthen my determination to speak up. It's like going on a diet. Saying I'm on one isn't enough to keep me from eating too much. I need a formal diet structure to control my food intake, just as I needed the push of a legal contract to maintain my resolve. If what you promise is going to affect your life, you better mean what you agree to. You sure learn about yourself in the process.

*Plain English, please.* Legal premarital contracts can be user friendly; they do not have to be written in legalese. Bob and I insisted on the use of personal pronouns and our first names rather than party-of-the-first-part jargon. We also made sure that all legal terms were put into plain English.

## *Choice: No covenant at all

States used to view marriage in only one way, traditionally: the husband is the breadwinner, the wife is the homemaker, the couple is monogamous, and the marriage lasts forever. Now, states, recognizing that there are different marital structures, have altered their regulation books so that past gender assigned responsibilities are allocated in neutral terms. Still, the state decides how marriages should function. That is, unless you write your own marital plan. If you do not create a prenuptial agreement that is legally binding, your state's choices rule (See the chapter "But Why A Legal Contract?").

## *Flexible spine; not rigid, not weak*

Your covenants set your rules. Fundamental to the intimate contracting process, however, is how flexible partners are as they work through to their solutions. Since we cannot predict what will take place in our lives, an adaptable attitude before, during, and after premarital contracting needs to be established. Flexibility can be built into your premarital contracts.

## *You have the right to change your contracts

Couples have every right to update their covenants, but they also have a responsibility to do so with care so as not to cancel any conditions they want to keep. You can include a clause for periodic review. Your private, as well as legal covenants can include a statement such as attorney M. Dee Samuels suggests:

> "We are going to redo this agreement in five years (annually, monthly) to assure ourselves it is what we want. We agree that we will attempt to make changes that meet our current needs if they seem to be desirable."

A lawful premarital contract can also be revised once a couple is married. In fact, after Bob and I moved to Washington (our marriage took place in New Mexico and our legal prenuptial agreement was signed and sealed in New Jersey), we renewed our contract to ensure its validity—and made updates and changes too—in the form of a Postnuptial Property Settlement. After all, not only had we changed state residency, but we moved from an equitable distribution jurisdiction to one of community property. We wanted to make sure our new contract would conform with Washington State's requirements, so we looked for an attorney who was familiar with marital agreements and estate planning. As with our prenuptial agreement, we made sure to fulfill the conditions necessary to satisfy us and the state that our contract is legally in effect.

## *You have the right to disagree

There will be conflicts between partners as they engage in the premarital contracting process just as there will be in their life together. Some couples have created conflict resolution options just in case.

> Stan and Roberta established a mediation format. They talked about which of their friends they both had confidence in, picked one, and spoke with her. Would she agree to mediate disputes if necessary? Their friend was uncomfortable with that responsibility and requested that they choose two other people as well. Now Roberta and Stan have a three-member mediation support system, which, by the way, they haven't needed to call on during their seven years of marriage.

Couples might want to list in their agreement some conditions for settling disputes on their own. For example, routinely taking a ten minute break or a day to think things over when discussions get too hot gives distance to help clear heads, yet still keeps decision deadlines in mind. Another method might be to assign who has the final say for certain decisions: one partner holds the deciding vote on children matters while the other has the last word on financial choices. Or the partners might take turns on who has the final responsibility for a particular category.

## *You have the right to determine the life of your covenant

Lovers may set a time limit on their covenants. Burt, the affluent man described in the chapter "Is Hot Love A Cold Business?", believed that if his marriage with Rita lasted ten years he could trust that she married him for himself, not his wealth. Their contract had a self-destruct, termination clause. Another couple felt that if, after five years of marriage, they could rely on working things out spontaneously, they did not want their contract to be valid beyond that time. Bob's and my prenuptial agreement, for example, had to last since certain property arrangements for the children by our first marriages went counter to marital estate regulations and unless they were supported by our legal contract they might not be fulfilled.

## *How do we start one of those things?*

Preparing your premarital contract is not a one-time activity or even a short period endeavor. It is a long-term commitment. Six months before you marry is a good time to begin your intimate contracting, if you haven't done so before then.[3] Whichever types of covenants you decide to use, premarital contracting is a powerhouse way for lovers to really get to know each other. Its inherent process will make each of you think and rethink how you would handle situations that may come up as your marriage grows.

Since you will be dealing with the most important issues you may face in your relationship, let alone your life, give yourselves time to go through premarital communication in the most supportive way. Space to think and discuss, discuss more and think more, and still more will bring returns triple fold. Rushing through your contracting to sign an agreement that you are not fully satisfied with will cause resentment and distrust. Couples and their families expend incredible amounts of effort and money to make their wedding ceremonies special. How long is your ceremony going to be? Perhaps twenty minutes? Romantic it can be, meaningful it is, but in importance to the rest of your life together, the ceremony pales in comparison to saving your marriage ahead of time with premarital contracting.

## *Do you have a premarital contracting principle?

The credo you and your partner evolve will establish the atmosphere of your contracting. Bob's and my strategy was (and still is)—to respect each other's autonomy. It helped us focus and refocus during our sessions when issues became muddled by our emotions. We

---

3. See *The Ideal Schedule For Prenuptial Agreement Completion* in the Appendix.

knew we loved each other; we reaffirmed that daily and during our contracting sessions. But we needed our strategy to help us create a prenuptial agreement that, rather than being a divorce-decree-in-advance, set forth the basic principles of our marriage.

## *Wake up call: act on your lists

There are two types of fact-gathering that will take place based on your joint pre-premarital contract lists. You will collect concrete particulars that you need to make decisions covering such items as bank accounts, stocks and bonds, personal possessions, and debts; perhaps a student loan or a mortgage. The sorting of that kind of information just takes time. You may have to get an appraisal, collect statements of accounts, or locate insurance policies.

The not-so-easy information gathering—deciding what you want—takes thought, communication, adjustment, rehashing, and, finally, agreement. You probably will consider lifestyle issues that range through such subjects as future career goals, children, who does which work, vacations, where to live, money issues, and, last but not least, hobbies. This stage challenges you and your partner to create, and then, to begin to commit to mutually acceptable solutions. The questions at the end of the previous chapters of this book have stimulated your experimentation with different premarital contracting and negotiation skills. Call on your communication muscles now. You can rely on them to assist you in these sessions. Do not expect your decisions to be made in one sitting. Some may of course, but there will be other issues that, as you and your partner search for answers, will stretch your communication skills.

There are certain concerns that can be resolved only by your searching and delving into what you need to be happy. Other situations can benefit from the use of expert advice. Experts, since they are not personally involved in your issues, can be an excellent, unbiased resource. The chapter "Whose Contract Is This Anyway?" offers a review of experts who may be of help as you proceed in your prenuptial contracting.

## *Decision time: Which covenants do we want to use?*

You are creating your own marriage. You may use whatever type of pledges you want to, limited only by your imagination, your will to speak up, and the support of your love.

During a trip to the south, a friend introduced me to Diane, a writer, and her husband Jake. Over coffee we described our writing projects. The topic of my book sparked more than a discussion of writing techniques. To my delight, Diane and Jake had five premarital covenants, only one of which was a formal, lawful, prenuptial agreement.

Diane told me, "We needed to have a premarital contract to legally bind certain financial arrangements. For example: our marital home had been mine before we married." Diane believed, and Jake was happy that she did, that her home, soon to be their conjugal space, should become their joint property. Diane continues, "But what if our marriage ended? My major asset—the house—would have become joint property. My asset value would be cut in half."

They used a legal prenuptial agreement to secure their solution. It stated that if their marriage ended within five years the whole value of the house (appraised as of the date of their marriage) was Diane's property. After five years of marriage, half the value was hers, the other half was Jake's. During that time, funded by Jake's income, they would be improving the value of their home. They agreed that by the end of five years, they would have equal equity in the house.

Jake and Diane told me about their four lifestyle covenants too. They did not feel that these contracts required legal support. As Diane explains, "What holds these covenants together and keeps them working is our commitment to them." Each contract concentrated on a particular area. One covered all their plans regarding raising children, including how many they would have and which religion to be followed. Another covenant set out their commitments in support of their careers and covered relocation, sabbaticals, and retirement. The third covenant dealt with their personal interests such as hobbies, friends, and relatives. This contract also delineated responsibility for their elderly parents, just in case. The fourth contract focused on household responsibilities such as cleaning and cooking, and allotment of private retreat spaces.

Jake adds, "We knew our requirements would change, so even though we tried to keep our covenants fairly general, we felt a yearly review of each contract was important. Plus, we enjoy going over our commitments and pledges."

## Which troths will you pledge?

We are in a cultural age where the variety of marital options is extensive and limited only by our wishes. Your marriage need not be controlled by outside judgments; it can be created by your and your mate's dreams. How you and your lover pledge your troth is up to you. Be active and you create your marriage; be inactive and your home state controls your fate.

### Where do we begin talking this time?
Your *whys* make your lover wise!

- Do you feel as morally committed to the pledges you make to your partner as you do to business promises?
- Has your trust in your mate grown?
- What do you want your covenant to cover?
- Are you afraid you'll lose the romance of your love?
- Why are you contracting?

### Discussion starter:

- Pledge your love to each other in new ways.

For those of you who would like to do some additional reading on the subject of this chapter:

*Don't Get Married Until You Read This: A Layman's Guide To Prenuptial Agreements*, David Saltman, J.D., L.L.M. and Harry Schaffner, J.D.

*Justice, Gender, And The Family*, Susan Moller Okin

*Man's World, Woman's Place: A Study in Social Mythology*, Elizabeth Janeway

*The Marriage Contract: Spouses, Lovers, and the Law*, Lenore J. Weitzman

*Women And Home-Based Work: The Unspoken Contract*, Kathleen Christensen

# 7 But Why A Legal Contract?

*Choose to be responsible for defining your marriage.*

> He that lives upon hope will die fasting.
>
> BEN FRANKLIN

Would you obey an outsider who told you where to spend your money?

Are you willing to work as hard as you do now for less pay?

Would you listen to a stranger ordering you how to run your life?

DID ANY LOVER out there say "Yes."? Will any of you say "No!" to these questions? If you don't speak up, your state decides your marital roles and rules. When you and your lover pledge "I do" at your wedding ceremony you have agreed to a legal contract with conditions ordered by your state. Generally, unless premarital couples have prepared their marriage contracts, they do not really know what they have legally bound themselves to. Instead, we find out what our unspoken, lawful, spousal benefits and obligations are only at widowhood or divorce.

You have the right to create your own marital blueprint; one that reflects cultural expectations, your personal goals, or a unique combination. If you don't accept the responsibility that goes with this right—to define the structure of your marriage—your states does.

### *The primary reason for a premarital contract: To design your own marriage*

Sylvia Law, Professor of Family Law,[1] says, "The premarital contracting process alerts you to the fact that the law may not do what you would do for yourself." I also am convinced of the need for lovers to be responsible for their interests, but my education came through life experience, not law school. The traditional world I lived in, first as a child and then later as a single parent, viewed independent women as unnatural. This attitude forced me to face a dichotomy within myself. On one side of the fence sat the me who had been trained to be taken care of in return for services rendered, and on the side I preferred perched the me who cared for herself and related with family and friends as she chose to.

### *Backbone support

Life had taught me that economic security was essential for me to remain independent. Contemplating marriage after choosing to remain single for many years, I wondered how to keep my hard-won autonomy. Slowly, an idea formed. Bob and I could use a premarital covenant to notify us, our children, and perhaps the state how we would integrate the management of our incomes and assets into our partnership.

Bob's eyes opened wide when I suggested that we write a prenuptial agreement. Although he didn't say so, I assumed he felt hurt. At the time though, I was too afraid to find out because my resolve to contract issues through was, at best, shaky. I needed the impersonal, concrete aspects of a legal contract to give me the backbone to resist external and internal messages: don't

---

1. Professor Sylvia Law teaches at New York University Law School.

talk about assets because you might seem too pushy—women should not be aggressive. Don't threaten your mate's ego—we shouldn't hurt the ones we love; and anyway, men's egos are more fragile than everyone else's. Don't be selfish—women must think of others before themselves.

It was during these initial discussions about possessions and resources that Bob and I realized that we were actually creating the structure of our marriage. Unexpectedly, these talks had broadened to include our deepest expectations, dreams, and needs.

## *Your marriage; your design*

Incredible as it may seem, many premarital couples enter their marriage not knowing what they bind themselves to in the eyes of the law. Most of us think of marriage as a culmination of our romance, but it is also a beginning of our new life together. It is not without constraints, however. State regulations determine a married couple's behavior and responsibilities. You may think that your love is unique, but your state doesn't know that unless you tell it so through a prenuptial agreement. The purpose of a premarital contract is to clarify two levels of your marriage structure: how you and your lover want to relate, and how you both want your marriage to be regarded by the state.

## *Your state's definition of marriage, or yours?*

It is important to remember that most of our marital regulations developed in times far different from those we live in now. Fortunately, we are in changing times and there are many options open to us. Our cultural boundaries have become more flexible and our socioeconomic structures are being redefined. Nadine Taub, Professor of Law, observes, "As individuals work through their answers to these [marital lifestyle] questions for themselves, their insights may lead to guidelines and practices that courts will eventually adopt."[2] To widen the scope of legal marital provisions, we must become knowledgeable about what the current requirements are, as well as take an active role in speaking out about what we do like and what we don't want.

## Know your state's views on marital property

There are two fundamental marital property systems: common law and community property. "In merging the couple's assets, the **community property system** emphasizes the couple's unity or partnership, while the **common law system** underscores the independence of the two spouses by allowing them to hold their property individually."[3]

## *Community property states

Overall, income or assets acquired during the marriage by either spouse (except inheritances or gifts) belong to both in community property states. Assets can include your home, other real estate, stocks, bonds, savings, future salary, and income gained from investments. Community property jurisdictions are: Arizona, California, Idaho, Louisiana, Nevada, New Mexico, Texas, Washington, and Puerto Rico. Within the two marital property systems each state has its own permutations, and the distinction between community property and common law is sometimes crossed. Although not a community property state, "Wisconsin, because of legislation that took effect in 1986, treats income earned and property acquired during marriage as jointly owned."[4]

---

2. Professor Nadine Taub, co-author of *The Law of Sex Discrimination*, teaches at the School of Law-Newark, Rutgers, The State University of New Jersey. She is also connected with the Women's Rights Litigation Clinic at the S.I. Newhouse Center for Law and Justice.

3. Professor J. Ralph Lindgren and Professor Nadine Taub; *The Law Of Sex Discrimination*; West Publishing Co.; St. Paul; 1988; p. 318.

4. American Bar Association, Public Education Division; *Your Legal Guide to Marriage and Other Relationships*; "You and the Law Series"; 1989; p. 22.

## *Common law states

Generally, the separate property system used in the past by the forty-two common law states held that whichever spouse had title to the property, owned it. However, Professor Taub points out, "Common law states have come to adopt the 'equitable distribution' method. Upon divorce, assets are allocated according to the parties' present needs and circumstances and their past contributions to the marriage." Nonetheless, equitable distribution does not mean equal distribution. As well, "Considerable differences remain in the states' views as to whether only 'marital' property is, or both 'marital' and 'separate' property are, before the court for division."[5]

### *Know your state's views on financial responsibilities*

Learn how your state will regulate your assets if you don't. Find out how its property laws will touch your specific affairs: children born of a prior marriage, possession and control of your family's business, or income from your salary or from investments you or your spouse made before your marriage and will continue to make afterward. Your state determines the ownership of your assets as soon as you begin your marriage; it does not wait until you or your mate dies or you go through a divorce.

### *Your views on your state's views*

How you and your mate want to handle your money may very well be in conflict with conditions your state imposes. Ownership distinctions are not limited to property lines, after all, they permeate your living marriage. If only one of you owns the family home, are both

---

5. Harry Krause, Esq.; *Family Law In A Nutshell,* Second Edition; West Publishing Co.; 1986; Section 26.3, "Equitable Distribution, Division of 'Marital Property' and the UMDA" (Uniform Marriage and Divorce Act).

of you equal partners in your marriage? Do you want to invest yourself in the connubial nest if it isn't yours? When only one of you controls the purse strings, do you both participate in charting the course of your partnership? Are there alternatives that may more comfortably suit you and your mate?

## *You own, I own. What do we own?

Many lovers are saying "No!" to the question, "Would you obey an outsider (in this case, your state) who told you where to spend your money?" Instead, couples are creating premarital covenants because they want to control the future ownership. They want to control their individual and jointly held resources.

> While we sit in her sun-filled, country-style kitchen drinking freshly brewed coffee, Rita reminisces about the emotionally trying premarital contracting she went through with Burt seven years ago. (As mentioned in the previous chapter, Burt and Rita's premarital contract self-destructs after they have been married for ten years.) She describes how difficult it had been to convince Burt that she loved him, not what he had. "He was really hung up about 'his' money. Since Burt was a kid, he had been taught that he could have whatever he wanted if he could pay for it. His money was part of his self-image and he was frightened of losing control."

Typically, in our society men have been more concerned than women about protecting their property. Now, though, women are also accruing assets and many feel as territorial as Burt does. To determine how you want to set up your mutual financial arrangements, explore your feelings about your possessions. Are presumed gender roles dictating your expectations, or are you? Learn what is real for you and your lover, and which of your state's arbitrary marital and personal property "shoulds" you want to avoid.

"Equitable distribution and community property laws, which no longer guarantee a spouse sole ownership of property simply because his or her name is on it, is one reason for the growing prevalence of prenuptial agreements."[6] It is up to premarital couples to identify what they want to commingle and what they want to keep defined as their separate property before they marry, and, with a prenuptial agreement, uphold their arrangements once they marry.

### *Money is a survival tool in our world

Yet, it is difficult for many spouses who work in their mate's business to ask for a salary.

> Patricia tells me, "My fiance doesn't pay me for the bookkeeping I do for his shop. But he sure takes me on great vacations." Working part time in a Minneapolis cafe, she has been spending more and more hours at Tod's garage maintaining his books. She has gotten quite good at bookkeeping, but she recalls, "When I first started, I didn't know what I was doing. His dad showed me how to keep the records. It took me a year to learn everything. I owe them for teaching me. Once we marry it will be different." "How?" I ask her. She is not sure how.

One's psyche is nourished by knowing that you can earn income and survive. When Patricia and Tod marry, what arrangements will they set up so that her skills and input will be counted too? Economic realities can cause intense conflict between each of you, or between you as a couple and your families. By discussing your financial plans ahead of time, you and your mate can clarify how you plan to handle one of the most emotionally weighted devices of our society.

### *You owe, I owe. What do we owe?

Payment of the debts one or both of you incurred prior to your marriage is another issue to discuss before you marry. "Generally, neither

---

6. Gail J. Koff, Esq.; *Love and the Law*; Simon and Schuster; New York; 1989; p. 91.

spouse is responsible for the premarital debts of the other."[7] As a first step to organize your money issues, each of you can put together financial statements listing your individual assets and liabilities. Once you have the whole picture you can more easily determine how you plan to pay off debts. Will you be jointly responsible, or will each of you pay off your own debts? When? How? Debts after you marry are treated according to the property system of the state you reside in. "Generally speaking, however, in most states just being married does not give one spouse the right to load the other with debts."[8]

## *Pledge economic support for your future too

There are situations unique to each couple that warrant attention. For example, if you expect to go for further professional training but put your plans on the back burner while you support your mate's education, you may want to know how your state and sweetheart evaluate your contribution. Do your endeavors translate into tangible benefits for you in the future? If so, how? If not, why not? What value do you place on your efforts?

## *Know your views and your states' views on child rearing*

Bringing up our own children is not a service we expect to be paid for, even when most of the responsibility falls on one parent. But paradoxically, in our culture what is paid for is valued. Raising children is hard work and the truth of the matter is that it doesn't put money in the family's pocketbook. Premarital couples may want to study the value they put on raising their children. Ask yourselves whether you would agree to work as hard as you do now for less pay for any reason other than raising your children? Can the caregiver value his home work without the measurement of income?

---

7. Steven Mitchell Sack; *Complete Legal Guide; Marriage, Divorce, Custody, & Living Together*; Fisher Books; 1987; p. 58.
8. *Your Legal Guide To Marriage—and Other Relationships*; p. 23.

Will the income earner value the caregiver's efforts as much as her own?

Peter and Brenda invited me to their Manhattan, co-op apartment to talk about their child-rearing choices. Brenda, an attorney, had been with a major law firm in the city. She interrupted her career to raise their children, a decision she and her husband Peter made together. This Saturday morning we are in the living room enjoying their daughter Janey's reactions to the cheerful sounds her brightly colored toys make as she plays. Brenda, in jeans and T-shirt, looks relaxed and happy sitting cross legged on the floor. While rolling a strange looking wooden animal back and forth to Janey, she says, "I knew I would be working as hard caring for my children as I had at my office, but somehow when Peter and I made plans that revolved around money decisions, money I no longer helped bring in, I was really uncomfortable."

Brenda wanted to be an equal partner in family decisions, so she had to make sure that her child-care work was as valued as her professional work had been. Peter agreed with her. Their solution was supported by their premarital contract in which they stated that Peter's earned income was made possible because of their joint efforts. Each, therefore, had the responsibility and authority to determine how their money was used.

Peter leans forward on the soft, gray, corduroy-covered couch. He has a youthful exuberance that must serve him well in his advertising career. His effervescent manner belies the heaviness of his concerns; concerns that also influenced what went into their premarital contract. He says, "If I hadn't been convinced that Brenda would go back to work once the children were old enough not to need her attention full time, I would have had serious hesitation about starting a family. Her income contributed to a lifestyle I didn't want to give up. The thought of supporting a family totally by myself was overwhelming."

States are beginning to recognize the different marital role options that exist now in our society. But, although new models have been acknowledged, Peter felt burdened by the traditional expectation that the male must be his family's economic provider.

On the other hand, since Brenda had agreed to step away from her career for the sake of their children, she needed economic assurances too. Brenda and Peter's premarital contracting helped them resolve his worries as well as hers.

To fulfill her agreement to contribute financially to their marriage and also to keep her professional expertise marketable, Brenda hopes to find some part-time consulting jobs while she is the primary caregiver for their children. She will go back to practicing law full time once the children are all in grade school. The cutoff point for Brenda's child-care leave of absence from full-time work has been left open to ensure flexibility in responding to each child's needs.

## *I am marrying you, not the state*

This chapter's third opening question asks, "Would you listen to a stranger ordering you how to run your life?" Posed another way, it questions lovers, "Do you really want your state to control how your marriage is structured?" Professor Marjorie Maguire Shultz describes what the state's view of marriage has been: "Monogamous; and women stay home and men go to work."[9] That is not necessarily a wrong view of marriage, but it is important to ascertain whether it is your view. Once engaged couples identify what they are willing to agree to for their marriage, they would be wise to find out whether their decisions fit in with their state's positions. If not, a legally binding contract is in order.

## *Vive la différence?

Although traditional gender measurements have begun to loosen, they still exist to different degrees in courts, in businesses, in schools; and they linger in personal relationships. Their influences on our

---

9. Professor Marjorie Maguire Shultz teaches Contract Law at Boalt Hall School of Law, University of California.

lives remain, and are often accompanied by, a bias that tends to favor males. Our Social Security system is a prime example of the tenacity of gender preferential attitudes. Professors Taub and Lindgren describe the unfair mind-set of these regulations, "As her husband's dependent rather than his partner, a widow receives only part of her deceased spouse's benefit."[10]

RETIREMENT, a Social Security Administration handbook dated January 1988, describes what retirees can expect, "Benefits also can go to a divorced spouse at sixty-two or older if the marriage lasted ten years or more." Why don't wives divorced before the ten-year watermark deserve benefits? Most often, it is during the early years of marriage that women work less so that they can care for their children more. When a woman takes time off from the paid work force to raise her children, "On her savings record [for Social Security benefits], zero earnings will be entered for those years, thereby further reducing her benefits."[11]

## *Are we equal partners?

To modify gender prescribed marital regulations, Family Law statutes are being written in neutral language. Unfortunately, such terms "frequently obscure the fact that so much of the real experience of 'persons,' so long as they live in gender-structured societies, *does* in fact depend on what sex they are."[12] Gender roles give us different, and in many cases unequal survival skills.

## *Withdrawal pains

Important to note, "By far the most important property acquired in the average marriage is its career assets."[13] One's career, however,

---

10. Lindgren and Taub; *The Law of Sex Discrimination*; p. 321.

11. Ibid., p. 321.

12. Susan Moller Okin; *Justice, Gender, And The Family*; Basic Books, Inc., Publishers; New York; 1989; p. 11.

13. Ibid.; p. 163.

is more than an asset; for many of us it is emotional sustenance, promising security, acknowledging capability, guaranteeing survival. Yet not surprisingly, most often the wife is the one who chooses to be the primary child caregiver at the cost of her career, while the husband continues to develop his career.

Recently, I spoke with a group of college women about premarital contracting. Although they each plan to develop careers for themselves, most intend to be the caregiver for their children as well. I asked them why they expect to be the partner responsible for the children and I was surprised by their answers. The consensus was that they *should* be. One young woman explained, "It just seems natural." Another added, "I don't want anyone else raising my kids." Only one admitted, "I might let my husband participate in bringing up my children." We still have a long way to go in erasing gender determined behavior.

## *Pains of reentry

Whether because of free choice, a divorce settlement, or widowhood, when women reenter the work force, they face high hurdles: heavy duty catch-up games; pay disproportionately low in comparison to what men receive; and, for many women, single parent responsibilities. The price these barricades extract from women hurt their men. You and your partner can set up your own non-gender-defined marital structure that recognizes the realities of your partnership. This is not in preparation for divorce, but a necessity for your marriage. Gender bias issues exist and it is up to us to balance those weights in our own lives.

## *The big "D"*

The primary reason for couples to draw up legal, premarital contracts is to clarify and establish their partnership. The couple's end goal is to have a happy and long-lasting marriage. Professor Law also reminds her Family Law students of another reason for contracting,

"The second important function of a premarital agreement is to save one pain and expense should there be a divorce."

## *Do the courts respect premarital contracts?

Courts around the country are recognizing prenuptial agreements as binding at the time of death or divorce. Since many current marriage alliances do not fit the traditional mold, conventional court solutions no longer suffice. Professor Shultz says, "To some extent we are recognizing private decisions because efforts to impose standardized public decision-making have simply fallen apart at the seams. The default mode in our society is 'when in doubt, let people make their own arrangements.' This is the norm in Contract Law." The courts, in doubt, prefer that people set their own terms. Attorney Richard Singer suggests another reason judges respect conditions set by prenuptial contracts. Facing the high numbers of divorce cases in their courtrooms, judges look to these contracts for guidance as they struggle to make decisions. Honoring prenuptial agreements speeds settlement time.

But the courts will back prenuptial agreements only as long as certain conditions are met. Ways to protect the validity of your contract are discussed in the chapters "What Makes A Contract A Contract?" and "Your Premarital Agreement." Since each state has its own statutes, it is important to review your contract with an attorney familiar with your local regulations. chapter "Whose Contract Is This Anyway?" discusses some uses and limitations of experts.

## *You or the judge can decide

When you create your premarital contract, you design the framework of your marriage. Are you equally dedicated to establishing, while you are in love, what you would agree to should the impossible happen? "Since judges are given considerable discretion in allocating property and determining [child and spousal] support obligations when divorcing parties cannot agree, premarital agreements can reduce certain financial uncertainties that might otherwise occur at the time of divorce."[14] If you do not want generic standards of marriage to dictate your marital structure, why acquiesce to a possible divorce settlement being decided by a judge who is a stranger to you and to whom you are unknown. Your values, your concerns, and your input to your marriage are only known to the court if you make them available. Otherwise, the judge, human like the rest of us, will make his decisions based on his perceptions. Your premarital contract edifies the court of your and your lover's intentions and agreements. It is equally necessary for you to know what the court will respect as reasonable in your prenuptial agreement.

## *The court's position on children

Since children are unable to care for themselves, the courts "reserve the right to determine the acceptability of clauses pertaining to children."[15] Any child custody and support arrangements you have included in your covenant will be carefully scrutinized. Nevertheless, your prenuptial agreement can influence the judge's decisions. For example, if, in your premarital contract, you have agreed to bring your children up with a particular religious background, the court will take that into consideration. Your premarital agreement will be followed only to the extent it meets the best interests of your children according to the court's measurements.

## *The court's position on spousal support

Many affluent or older lovers who are ready to join together in holy matrimony hesitate because they want to keep their individual estates for offspring of their prior marriages. It is legally okay, when one or both partners can financially take care of themselves, for spouses

14. *Your Legal Guide to Marriage*; p. 14.
15. Ronald C. Schmucker, Esq., partner in the law firm Perry & Schmucker located in Burlington, Vermont, specializes in Family Law.

to waive their rights to support. However, in case of divorce the court is interested in protecting any disadvantaged spouses. To that end the courts reserve their right to determine spousal support.

"The most popular contemporary spousal support is 'rehabilitative.' Rehabilitative support is based on the premise that a spouse who was economically dependent or disadvantaged during marriage should become an economically self-sufficient person."[16] Although age, length of marriage, and other factors are considered in awarding maintenance support, is a spouse who has spent her efforts on her family rather than developing marketable skills adequately compensated by neutral-gender, no fault divorce rules? You and your mate can set up your premarital contract to support each other in case of a divorce.

## *The court's position on property settlements

Courts will most likely honor the property conditions that you establish in your premarital contract as long as you and your mate gave an honest representation to one another of your financial standings, and their distribution is fair. For example, an arrangement almost certain to be followed by the court would be if both partners are affluent and agree to waive marital rights to each other's property.

## *The court's position on estate plans

Wills, without the backing of a legal premarital contract, can be contested. "In the absence of a prenuptial agreement, a surviving spouse may generally claim part of the estate regardless of the terms of the will. The amount that such an individual may claim is determined by state law."[17] If you want any arrangement other than your state's estate requirements, you must use a lawfully binding premarital or

---

16. *Your Legal Guide To Marriage*; p. 60.
17. Clint Willis; "Financial Vows In Remarriages," in the "Your Money" column of *The New York Times*; Saturday, March 5, 1988; p. 36.

marital agreement. Speak to your attorney about your state's testamentary requirements.

## *The court's position on your contract's validity

To have your prenuptial agreement withstand either a probate or a divorce court's scrutiny, there are three aspects that must be satisfied: One, both partners enter into the agreement freely and not under duress; two, there is full financial disclosure; and three, the prenuptial agreement does not promote divorce as a profitable option.

Additionally, certain states require that each of you has independent counsel. Even if it is not mandatory in your state to do so, it is in your best interests to have separate legal advice. Your lawyer can explain different aspects of the prenuptial agreement from your perspective. It is wise to be knowledgeable about what you are agreeing to, and understand all the ramifications. That way, when you sign your legal prenuptial agreement you will do so with full confidence and no resentment.

### *Contemporary choices: Cohabitation*

Partners who are living together unmarried because they want to try out their relationship before they marry; because the law does not recognize a gay couple's union as a legal marriage; or simply because they have chosen not to marry, must also protect their individual interests. Cohabitation contracts are as important to create as premarital contracts. Not only for the inherent communication benefits, but in addition, living-together mates do not have the protection marital rights offer. "However, cohabitants can make arrangements (sometimes called 'cohabitation contracts') that will be enforced and will give them similar rights, providing the agreements are not based upon sexual services and no policy precludes the courts from upholding such contracts."[18] There are important questions to find answers

---

18. Sack; *Complete Legal Guide: Marriage, Divorce, Custody, & Living Together*; p. 32.

to. For example, what happens to your joint property if one of you dies? Verify how you can protect yourself and your partner.

## *What is happening in your state?*

Actively determine what unspoken but legally binding conditions for marriage and cohabitation exist in your state. Don't placidly hope everything will turn out all right. You can locate attorneys who specialize in Family Law by contacting regional branches of such national organizations as the Association of Family Lawyers and the American Academy of Matrimonial Lawyers. Go to your county seat law library or local library and read the latest task force studies on women's rights and on gender bias issues in the legal system. Look at current bar and judicial reports. When you meet with your attorney, ask what standard regulations accompany a marriage certificate in your state.

## *But why a legal contract?*

"Where contracts are allowed, most states will enforce only 'express'[19] contracts. To be reasonably sure . . . negotiate a written contract with the help of independent legal counsel."[20] Perhaps the final proof of your premarital contract will be challenged by a divorce. We cannot forget that in the past years fifty percent of first marriages have ended in divorce; second marriages have a higher failure rate. But the primary purpose of negotiating prenuptial covenants is to preserve your marriage; and to do so lovers can encourage productive communication, and, through mutual respect, negotiation of issues. You can count on this process.

You have a choice. You can accept a set of rules for marriage established by your state, or determine your own. Being responsible

---

19. "An express contract is an actual agreement of the parties, the terms of which are openly uttered or declared at the time of making it, being stated in distinct and explicit language, either orally or in writing." *Black's Law Dictionary*, p. 171.

20. *Your Legal Guide to Marriage*; p. 18.

for yourself frees you and empowers you. Accountability gives you your own marriage.

### Where do we begin talking this time?
The *whys* make your lover wise!

- Do you know how you want to handle your income?
- Does your mate want to keep her premarital assets separate from yours?
- What joint marital property will you have?
- Whose last name do you want to use? Which last name will your children have?
- Do you know what your state's answers are to:
  Your assets and income questions
  Your child support questions

### Other state marriage regulations you may want to research:

### Legal domicile:

In many states a wife's legal domicile is determined by her husband's residence. This may have an impact on your income taxes, voting privileges, driver's license, state school tuition, or job requirements. Will this cause you problems?

### Property rights:

- Spousal consent: Do you want the right and responsibility of consent if your home is to be mortgaged or sold?
- Credit: Is your credit established? What credit history do you have? Do you need your marriage assets to obtain credit? Will your state recognize that you are half-owner of your marriage assets?

*Discussion starter:*

- What kind of wedding ceremony do you want to have?

For those of you who would like to do some additional reading on the subject of this chapter:

*A Legal Guide for Lesbian and Gay Couples,* Hayden Curry and Denis Clifford
*Complete Legal Guide: Marriage, Divorce, Custody, & Living Together,* Steven Mitchell Sack
*Family Law In A Nutshell,* Professor Harry D. Krause, Esq.
*Love And The Law,* Gail J. Koff
*State by State Guide to Women's Legal Rights,* NOW Legal Defense and Education Fund, P. O. Box 561, NY, NY 10013
*The Family Law Dictionary,* Robin D. Leonard and Stephen R. Elias
*The Law of Sex Discrimination,* Professor of Philosophy J. Ralph Lindgren and Professor of Law Nadine Taub
*The Living Together Kit,* Toni Ihara and Ralph Warner
*Your Legal Guide to Marriage and Other Relationships,* American Bar Association, Public Education Division
*Wills* (brochure) and *Planning For Life and Death* (booklet) free from Order Fulfillment, American Bar Association, 750 N. Lake Shore Drive, Chicago, IL 60611

# 8 *Whose Contract Is This Anyway?*

*Use experts as guides, not as authority figures to obey.*

> Do not be bullied out of your common sense by the specialist; two to one, he is a pedant.
>
> OLIVER WENDELL HOLMES, SR.

Do you always follow other people's advice?

Are you the type who always has an opinion?

Can you make final decisions?

"JUST MIND YOUR own business. Don't tell me what to do," a college friend of mine used to say when anyone dared offer her some advice. My theory about other people's ideas was and is that I am willing to listen to what they have to say, but then I decide what I want to do. Of course, it always depends on who is giving the advice, and whether I respect them or even want to know their opinions. But in the act of listening there is opportunity to learn something new, perhaps get an idea worth developing, or at the very least discover one route not to follow.

## *Experts see the parts; you see the whole*

We live in an age of specialization. There are rules, regulations, conditions, and a multitude of perplexing components for almost anything we want to connect with. It helps couples who are planning to write a premarital contract to have a professional's concentrated knowledge at their disposal. But you are the expert who sees the whole picture of your life. You know the most about yourself, despite what your parents may think.

## *Read the label for directions*

Whether you plan to have a verbal, informally written, or lawfully executed contract, you can get information and direction from many available resources. Money issues can be clarified by accountants, legal requirements explained by attorneys, and communication problems eased by counselors. Nevertheless, the decision premarital couples have to make is not limited to when to use an expert. You must also determine how to make the best use of their expertise. The final goal is to have experts help you achieve your goals, not to have them tell you what you want. Contracting partners do not have to know everything about everything; we just have to know enough to choose appropriate experts, and use them efficiently.

## *The take-care-of-me trap

Jennifer, a thirty-four-year-old, newly divorced mother of two, relates how she learned to take care of herself while dealing with experts—her divorce attorneys. "I went through four different lawyers before my divorce was final. Looking back, I think that I was overwhelmed by the temptation to let them do all the work. I didn't have a grip on what I wanted. But deep inside, I must have known something was wrong."

She describes her escape from relying too much on experts, "My first lawyer was a patriarch. 'Don't worry,' he'd tell me, his soothing voice patting me on my head, 'I'll take care of everything.' At first his method was very reassuring. But I soon realized that no matter how I tried I could not get a direct answer from him. My second lawyer was incredibly encouraging. 'You and the kids won't have to change your way of living,' he promised. Of course, his results were far removed from his promises. The third lawyer managed to have the worst characteristics of numbers one and two. Each lawyer, by the way, was recommended to me by friends, and I accepted their recommendations without question."

Fortunately, life's experience is a great teacher and Jennifer was a good student. She says, "By the time I met my fourth lawyer, I definitely knew the score. I had a long list of questions to ask him." This lawyer worked well enough, given the divorce route Jennifer had to follow. "Even so," Jennifer says, "I consulted with a fifth lawyer, using her as a measuring stick to check the reality of each situation I faced in my divorce proceedings."

Jennifer has just recently started to date. She is quite clear about what she will do if she ever marries again. "There is no question but that I'd want a premarital agreement. After going through my divorce, I want to make sure of certain things before I commit myself to another marriage."

## Parallel construction

No matter which type of expert, the process of identifying who you want to use will be the same.

## Who chooses whom?

To begin your search for the right expert, speak to friends who have worked successfully with the kind of specialists you decide to employ. Recommendations from other professionals in the same field or related disciplines are good sources for names. Your local or county library has professional listings that can help launch your search. Once you have names of experts, make an interview appointment for a fact finding, introductory session. As a prospective client, you can use the interview to gather such basic information as what kind of person this specialist is, how she works, and what she charges. The expert will use the interview session to determine whether she wants to work with you too.

## When does all this happen?

Good timing is essential to complete your prenuptial agreement. To be caring of yourself, your relationship, and your frustration tolerance, leave space between steps. Remember, you will need to coordinate your consultants' input with your intimate negotiation. Ideally, six months[1] will give you room to complete everything. If you have less lead time between your decision to make a prenuptial agreement and your wedding date, don't let the scheduling hold you back. Do inform your specialists about your time constraints, but don't give up on your goals.

## Training plus style equals a good choice

It is important to check an expert's professional training and to find out about his experience in the field. But equally relevant to the success of your working with a particular expert is the way you, your mate, and he will relate, and the boundaries you and your mate set.

## *Your expert's personal style

Figure out the kind of individual you and your lover would like to collaborate with: someone who assumes total leadership, telling you what to do and you follow orders—a patriarch; someone who listens to you and sympathetically nods yes—a hand holder; or someone

---

1. See *The Ideal Schedule For Prenuptial Agreement Completion* in the appendix.

who pays attention to your details and gives you guidance—a consultant. Mix and match your own blend until you and your partner have a sense of the advisory approach you want your specialists to have. Your experts have to be willing to hear your information; you have to be able to communicate it.

## *Your expert's boundaries

Professionals tend to see things from the perspective of their expertise. Specialized training, however, can limit experts in an important way; they may disregard what they think are extraneous factors. Diane's transfer of individual ownership of her home to joint ownership by Jake and her, discussed in the chapter "In This Troth Do We Pledge?", illustrates that there is more than meets one expert's eyes. Their accountant or lawyers might not have put as much importance as Diane did on how Jake would feel living in her home. Yet, his feelings were a motivating force for Diane. A therapist, while understanding Diane's gesture of trust in the future of her and Jake's relationship, might not consider the tax implications of the transfer of home ownership. You and your lover will have to educate your accountant, lawyer, insurance agent, or family counselor to the essentials of your relationship.

## *Who's in charge here?

Put your specialist's personality and expertise together, and let the combination work for you. Make it clear to yourself as well as your consultant that you want them to guide, not take over. But they do need your input. An architect can design a beautiful house, but for it to be your home, you must give pertinent information about your lifestyle, your values, your goals, your likes and dislikes. The same is true of the experts you will use to clarify your premarital contracts. Don't assume that these professionals (they are not gods) can determine what is best for you. They are influenced by their life experiences, dreams, and training to see things in certain ways. They can expand their vision to see your view too. Your expert only advises; you decide.

## If you need to go to a lawyer, you must be in trouble

We are living in a litigious society. But suing others is not the only reason lawyers are employed. Many jokes to the contrary, attorneys' skills can guide clients to create positive results and avoid problems. What do you talk about? Tell your attorney what your goals are, then he will give you information. Can your goals be fulfilled? If so, how? If not, what else can you do?

### *Talk about an estate plan

An attorney who has knowledge of estate planning, tax, and Family Law can direct premarital partners how to protect their heirs.

Ruth, my friend's mom whom we met earlier in the chapter "What's There To Talk About?", was hurt by her second husband George's one-sided attempt to assuage his children's concern about their inheritance. Instead of being stingy, had George protected the legacy his children expected with an estate plan, he would have benefited two ways. His duty to his children fulfilled, he could have been generous to Ruth and himself. Additionally, Ruth and his children might have had more of a chance to like each other.

If you already have an estate plan, it will need to be revised once you marry; and it would be wise to buttress your plan with a prenuptial agreement. Speak with your attorneys for appropriate instruments, such as trusts, to support your goals. Wills need to be updated too. "We just need a simple will, nothing complicated," Ruth and George had said to their lawyer. Not necessarily so. The inheritance that the surviving spouse is legally allowed is determined by state law. If you want to override the state's requirements, a prenuptial agreement is required. Still and all, the state may not approve of an agreement that jeopardizes a spouse's financial security. As a part of the information needed to establish the fairness of your agreement, your lawyer will advise you and your mate to provide complete financial disclosure.

## *Talk about joint and separate property

Do you want to transfer your individual property—which will go to your heirs—to joint marital property—which would go directly to your spouse at the time of your death? What are the tax consequences if you do? What are the estate ramifications if you don't? Ask your attorney what other property issues she, you, and your mate ought to discuss.

## *Talk about prenuptial agreements

Your lifestyle covenants are important and wonderful to contract. The follow-through of these pledges depends on you and your partner. But if you have contracts that enter the realm of your state's control, whether because of detailed estate plans or a simple will, or for establishing financial support or for gifting purposes, it is critical that your premarital contract has power so that it will not be dismissed. A lawyer can put your premarital contract in proper legal form and make sure that the steps taken to create it adhere to Contract Law.

## *They can only come in the door, no farther*

We can take advantage of our lawyers' expertise and still be in charge of our premarital contract's intent. Bob and I did as much as we could on our own so as to limit the extent that our lawyers were involved in our premarital contracting process. Once we decided what issues we wanted to attend to we asked my attorney for a sample prenuptial agreement. We used its format as a model to follow in writing out our contract. Both Bob's lawyer and mine checked what we had written to make sure that the legal interpretation of our agreement corresponded to what we meant to say. This necessitated office visits, phone calls, redrafting by us and by our attorneys. Bob's lawyer advised him of his interests and my lawyer did the same for me. We listened to our lawyers' suggestions, but we made sure we were comfortable with each clause in our contract. We were careful not to loose sight of our objective: to have a loving covenant that protected each of us.

## You and your attorney work together

It can be difficult to resist the temptation to let your lawyer make the decision. After all, the issues you discuss involve the law. They may seem beyond your capabilities, but don't let go of your part in the process. The purpose of your premarital contract is for you and your lover to have a say in the structure of your marriage. After all the effort you have put into your intimate negotiation, don't give your decision-making power away. On the other hand, in the pursuit of maintaining control over your contract, don't lose your lawyer's advice.

## Required counsel

To make sure that both of you have had your interests explained before you sign your contract, many states will require that you and your mate each have independent legal counsel. Be forewarned that if you sign a contract that is not fair to you after hearing an attorney's explanations, the court may take the position that you signed it with knowledge and forethought. Unless what you agreed to is way out of proportion to the situation, your contract will most likely stand.

## Use your lawyer's advice

A number of attorneys I spoke with questioned whether women and men have an equal ability to take care of themselves in contracting situations. Their rational for this concern is, "In our culture, the woman—more concerned about the relationship and children than about finances—often acquiesces, even against her lawyer's advice, in whatever agreement the man proposes."[2] If you know that you or your mate has an inclination to give in, support each other's contracting attempts. Also, let your attorney know your hesitations about premarital contracting.

## Your lawyer's responsibilities

Your attorney is working for you. It is her responsibility to listen to your goals and to help you achieve them or advise you that they are not possible. Attorney Gary Skoloff[3] explains that premarital contract counseling "calls for a terrific about-face for lawyers," but, if your goals include having your contract reflect your love for each other then it behooves your lawyer not to make it adversarial.

It is also your attorney's duty to make sure that all the legal requirements for your contract are fulfilled. She also must make you aware of your statutory rights. Your lawyer is there to advise you about what is in your best interests, not just to give pat, routine answers. She can suggest creative solutions that will protect you and your lover. Don't accept less.

## How to find the right one for you

The Martindale-Hubbell Law Directory, located in many libraries, is a massive compendium of lawyers. Entries in it include valuable information about specific attorneys; it lists their specialties, their ratings, and their addresses. Lawyers who practice in family, estate,

---

2. Mary-Lynn Fisher* and Linda L. McFadden**; "Premarital and Remarital Mediation: Complementary Roles For Lawyers And Therapists"; *Journal Of Family Law*; Vol. 24, 1985–86; p. 454; *Associate Professor of Law; Loyola Law School; Los Angeles, California; **Private Practice in Psychotherapy; Los Angeles, California.

3. Gary Skoloff is Chairman-Elect of the Family Law Section of the American Bar Association (1990) and senior partner of the firm Skoloff and Wolfe in Livingston, New Jersey.

and tax law are the ones to look for. Call your local American Bar Association and ask for names of attorneys in the areas of specialization you need. Check with other local law associations too. Ask for names of attorneys who are active participants; they will most likely be more up to date on the latest developments. When someone recommends an attorney they have used, ask why? Is he supportive, is she a fighter? Does he work assertively, yet not cause rifts? Is she reticent about giving information to her clients? Cross-reference your findings until you pinpoint attorneys you want to interview.

### Getting to know your expert

The first session with your attorney is simply an introductory interview. Think about what you want to find out ahead of time. An interview technique that I have found useful is to write out my questions in advance. Leave space to record your interviewee's answers. Better still, tape the interview. If your mind is racing ahead thinking of what to ask next, or you are trying to remember how the lawyer responded to your last question, you can't hear the nuances of his answers.

Study how the attorney communicates things to you. Does she give clear explanations; "don't worry" assurances rather than facts; or unfathomable legal jargon? Ask to see samples of her prenuptial agreement. If she doesn't have one readily available, persist. Her assistant can black out the names of the contractors to protect their privacy. You want to see what you are buying. What kind of interpretation of legal requirements and clauses can you expect? How long is the process? How will she communicate with your partner's attorney?

### *So, how much is it going to cost?

Lawyers need information from their clients—what you hope to accomplish and what your requirements are—before they can determine fees. Cost and time questions will be better asked after you have given the attorney information. But they must be asked if you want to know. Some attorneys charge a fixed fee; others charge per hour. Some will include the interview session in their fee for your prenuptial agreement; others may not charge for your initial visit whether or not you hire them.

### *Getting to know you too*

Even though the purpose of your first session is to interview the attorney, it is necessary for you to give some information about yourself in order to get relevant feedback. Be candid. You might want to prepare an outline script before your meeting so that you can quickly relate the basic facts. Obviously, the details of your situation will be uncovered at additional meetings once you have engaged your attorney. Indicate your deadlines and make your requirements very clear. For example, you can establish at the interview session that your contract, as well as any interaction between your lawyer and your mate's lawyer is to be non-adversarial. Now is the time to let your attorney know that you want your contract written in plain English.

### *You hold the reins*

Once you and your partner have selected your attorneys, remain in control of your premarital agreement.

### *You can do the initial creation

You and your mate can put together your contracts in whatever narrative form you like. Bob and I followed a boilerplate we obtained from an attorney, but we altered every legalese word we found and put in friendlier words. Never fear, each of your attorneys will certainly have their say in the review process.

## *You can be knowledgeable

You also control the creation of your prenuptial agreement by becoming familiar with what a contract is, and specifically, what a prenuptial agreement requires. You don't have to be the expert, only an educated consumer. Ask questions; clarify unknowns. Remember, the final decisions are up to you.

## *Only you know what your goals are

Pension plans, estate plans and wills, insurance policies, a durable power of attorney in case one of you becomes incapacitated, joint and separate property transfers, and more can be accomplished with your lawyers' guidance. Be straightforward about your concerns and disclose your complete financial situation. Relevant information you have not told your lawyer may haunt you later.

## *A surprising source of support*

You and your lover may come face-to-face with apparently unsolvable differences. Rather than facing each other across a conference table flanked by your lawyers, you might try mediation. Family Law attorney Ronald Schmucker[4] explains, "A mediating attorney must not represent either partner, nor does he represent them both. He is, at that time, simply a mediator who happens to be an attorney, and there is, at that time, no attorney/client relationship." An attorney-therapist team is an effective combination of experts who can help you dissolve your problems. In a mediation setting the therapist can assist lovers in clarifying their issues by guiding their communication process; the impartial attorney can suggest appropriate legal solutions. The mediator facilitates the contracting process; you and your mate choose your goals and your actions.

---

4. Attorney Ronald Schmucker has frequently acted as a neutral attorney-mediator, alone and in conjunction with a therapist.

## *If you need to go to a therapist you must be crazy*

While you are in the ARP, one or both of you may resist working with a family therapist, constrained by the belief that to do so means your relationship is a failure. It doesn't. Family therapists help couples see their stumbling blocks more realistically. Lovers can work with a counselor individually or in joint therapy. Alone, you may be more willing to speak about things that frighten or worry you, about yourself as well as your relationship. In joint sessions, with the guidance of the counselor, you can see your mate's perspective, and she, yours. Family counseling is not an arena for complaints, but a place of genuine searching for factors that cause friction. Your counseling sessions can save your relationship.

## *Your counselor's responsibilities*

Your counselor is working on your behalf to guide you to insights about your relationship.

## *How to find the right one for you*

Use an approach like the one described earlier for locating attorneys. Search through such sources as professional associations, your friends, personal physicians, or clergy.

## *Getting to know them*

Introductory interview goals are similar no matter who the expert. You are seeking information. Ask questions: what philosophical approach does the therapist use to help his clients attain their goals? Observe the therapist's communication style. Make clear to the counselor whether you plan regular visits or just a limited number; that you are interested in joint sessions only, or that you and your partner might like to meet separately with him also. Find out what his fees will be.

### *You hold the reins*

You know why you are in your expert's office. Whether you are there to clear up obstructions, acquire self-knowledge, or improve mutual communication, it is up to you to make sure that you get what you want. In your counselor's office as in your attorney's, it is in your best interest to be as forthright as possible.

### *"Marriage may be the oldest form of merger and acquisition."[5]*

Your banker, accountant, insurance agent, or financial planner are repositories of information that can influence your financial choices. You and your mate may have old habits of dealing with finances that make it difficult to cooperate. When suggestions come from third party sources, emotionally laden responses that you and your partner may have locked into have a chance of disengaging.

### *You only need an accountant if you are rich*

Generally most of us think "accountant" when it is income tax time. Tax is a prime issue for anyone who has earned income or received money from their assets, but filing tax forms takes on added complication when you switch from individual to joint returns. Other issues can change your tax picture even more.

---

5. Margot Slade; 'Your Money' column; "How To Marry A Couple's Funds"; *The New York Times*; Saturday, July 1, 1989; p. 30.

## *Gifts

Diane gifted half her house to Jake, her new husband. But there are tax consequences to gifting. Diane was advised by her accountant to wait and transfer half ownership of her house once she and Jake married. "Most transfers pursuant to PAs [Premarital Agreements] will not incur estate or gift taxes if made while the parties are married."[6] This gift was declared in their premarital agreement along with an explanation of Diane's intent, the conditions of the transfer, and that it would only take place if the marriage occurred. You can use your accountant's expertise to determine which property would be better held jointly and which to leave as separately owned.

## *Financial Disclosure

Complete financial disclosure is an important aspect of your prenuptial agreement. Its legal purpose is to make sure you know one another's net worth and that whatever you agree to, for support in case of divorce or asset allocation upon death, you know full well what you are doing. Total disclosure is also an indication of the trust you have in each other.

Your accountant can help you complete your financial disclosure and substantiate the value you put on your business, home, or other properties. Martin Sobel, a Certified Public Accountant located in Miami Beach, Florida, recommends including more information on your list than just dollars and cents. Describe what kind of business you have and how you established its value. Sobel also alerts beginning professionals that their future earning capacity is an asset and should be included in their financial disclosure. Insurance policies and pension plans are assets too.

---

6. "Tax Planning In Premarital Agreements"; *DTExpert*; Volume II, Number 5; September/October 1987; p. 5.

## *Joint responsibility

Your accountant can be helpful in other areas as well. With her expertise to support you, you can define your responsibilities to yourself, each other, and for your marriage in financial terms. She can help you set up plans for the future, budgets for the present, and also prepare for those in-case-of scenarios you want to avoid.

### *You only need an insurance agent if you are old*

You are never too young for life insurance—if you have a specific need. For example, if you are relying on your spouse to support you while you complete your education, her death might cause financial problems. But find out if the life insurance benefits are worth the expense. Once you have children you may be interested in ensuring both you and your mate. If called on, life insurance can provide child support or assist your heirs when they have to pay estate taxes.

### *You only need a financial planner if you have a lot of assets*

Budgeting, savings, or plans for long term goals can all benefit from the suggestions of a trained financial planner.

> Lauren and Stewart had a situation that might have become a problem sometime in their future. They had agreed that Lauren would be their child's primary caregiver, but she was really concerned about losing future career opportunities since she wouldn't be active in her profession. Stewart respected her worry. They went to a financial planner who helped them set up a schedule to invest money for Lauren's future. Knowing that when she was ready to return to work Lauren could afford any necessary training, they both felt more at ease about their child-care arrangements.

## How to use your financial expert

Whichever financial specialist you are dealing with, he will need complete information. Once you have had your initial interview, ask your expert for a list of material he will require for your next meeting. Bob and I sent our reports before our next appointment so that the expert could review them ahead of time. That way, when we met we were all familiar with the relevant background information and our time was spent on discussion.

## Getting to know you and them

The routine for locating financial advisors is similar to other specialists. The questions to ask them are also similar: cost of their services, their time commitment, and what they will do for you are but a few. As usual, it is up to you to give your experts appropriate information. Remember why you are going through this process. "Consulting an expert allows the two people to form a financial partnership working toward common goals, instead of waging war over what belongs to whom."[7]

## No expert is an island; no lover stands alone

Mary and Paul wanted to make sure that their respective children and grandchildren received their inheritances. Their estate planning required the assistance of a lawyer who devised trusts to ensure who got what; an accountant to make sure of what costs Mary and Paul could bear; a financial planner to help program their investments; and an insurance agent to arrange for life insurance. Your experts can assist each other furthering your goals.

---

7. Margot Slade; "How To Marry A Couple's Funds"; Your Money column, *The New York Times*; July 1, 1989; p. 30. Quotes Judyth Headington McGee, Certified Financial Planner in Spokane, Washington.

## Don't bury your head in the sand

Ignoring hard questions is using the ostrich technique. Although you may not see the problem because you have chosen to avoid looking at it, the problem is still there. Avoiding the monster issue doesn't stop it from coming closer and closer until it finally overwhelms your relationship. If you look for information in the right places, tough questions can be answered.

### Where do we begin talking this time?
Your *whys* make your lover wise.

- Do you feel obliged to follow advice once you receive it?
- Do you hate lawyers?
- Does the thought of going to a family counselor make you feel that your relationship is a failure?
- Do you panic whenever you think of money?
- Are you willing to look at different solutions?

### Discussion starter:

- Where do you want to go for dinner after you meet with the accountant.

### Sources for information about experts:
Lawyers:
American Bar Association:
Family Law Section
Estate and Tax Law Sections
750 N. Lake Shore Drive
Chicago, IL 60611

American Academy of Matrimonial Lawyers
20 North Michigan Avenue
Suite 540
Chicago, IL 60602
(312) 263-6477

Family counselors:
American Association for Marriage and Family Therapy
1717 K Street, N.W.
#407
Washington, D.C. 20006
(202) 429-1825

American Family Therapy Association
2020 Pennsylvania Avenue, N.W.
Suite 273
Washington, D.C. 20006
(202) 994-9000

Academy of Family Mediators
P. O. Box 10501
Eugene, OR 97440
(503) 345-1205

Financial planners:
The Institute of Certified Financial Planners
Two Denver Highlands, 10065 East Harvard Avenue
Suite 320
Denver, CO 80231-5942
(303) 751-7600

American Institute of Certified Public Accountants
1211 Avenue of the Americas
New York, NY 10036
(212) 575-6200

For those of you who would like to do some additional reading on the subject of this chapter:

*The American Lawyer: When and How to Use One*, American Bar Association
*The Help Book*, J. L. Barkas. This book is available in most libraries. It gives sources of support for the family.
*Martindale-Hubbell Law Directory*, Martindale-Hubbell, Inc.

# 9 What Makes A Contract A Contract?

*Play by the rules so you win the game.*

If you have a bargain with a friend, let that bargain be well penned.

BEN FRANKLIN

Are contracts just for strangers?

Do you expect everybody to remember their promises?

Can you talk with your lover about issues that bother you?

"DOESN'T HAVING A prenuptial agreement mean we don't trust each other?" asks Marilyn, a twenty-three-year-old graduate student. She is not happy with the topic of conversation at the dinner table. After listening to her parents and me discuss the progress of this book, Harry, Marilyn's fiance, has begun asking questions about prenuptial agreements. The air surrounding Marilyn seemed to get more and more oppressive. Once again, it is time for me to explain how premarital contracting can be a positive communication tool for lovers, and how prenuptial agreements need not be divorce-decrees-in-advance. Premarital contracts work for lovers.

## *Contracts are everywhere*

Have you ever been married? If so, you have signed a marriage contract. Have you bought a car, or a television on credit? If so, you have signed a contract. If you are renting an apartment, you have signed a lease, another type of contract. To take out a mortgage or home equity loan you must sign a contract. Insurance policies are contracts. Credit card agreements are contracts.

Individuals, partners, small businesses, and corporations use legally binding contracts to attain the ends they want and to protect their interests. A contractual promise is backed by law, but only if the contract has satisfied legal requirements. That our laws enforce contracts encourages most of us to think carefully before we sign them.

## *What is a contract between two individuals?*

"A contract is formed when either two persons each promise to do something or one person makes a promise in exchange for another person's performance of an act."[1] Although not all contractual agreements are legally required to be put in writing, one's memory can fail. Written contracts graphically affirm the contractors' promises, and, recognizing that, states' statutes of frauds indicate which types of contracts are too important to rely solely on recollection. Contracts do not have to be sophisticated, many-paged documents; they can be as simple as their users direct them to be. Basically, there are two actions that take place between contractors: an offer and an acceptance.

One night, using the moonlight to see, Bob wrote a contract. We had been walking our land with Ned, a local businessman, planning some road work he would soon do for us. Bob, Ned, and I decided that it would be a good idea to be clear about our agree-

---

1. Stephen Elias, Esq.; *Make Your Own Contract: Simple Contracts For Personal Use*; Nolo Press; Berkeley; 1990; p. 1:2.

ment. Written on the back of a hardware store circular that Ned found in his truck, our contract listed what he would do and how much we would pay for his services—his offer and our acceptance of his offer. We each signed the contract to indicate our mutual agreement of the conditions listed. Made under the gaze of a full moon, written on a crinkled piece of paper, it was a contract nevertheless.

## The value of a written contract

Many of us started on the contracting road of high finance in early childhood. We borrowed money from friends or siblings for comics or bubble gum, having agreed to, sooner or later, pay them back. Often, we contracted with our parents to advance us our allowance for some vitally important purchase. How do you handle loans now? While five or ten dollars out of your pocket on a night out with workmates might not be much, any substantial amount of money you lend may call for some form of promissory note. Although it may be a friend or relative who is doing the borrowing, it is still worth the weight of your good relationship to record the transaction in writing. You can include all the conditions of the loan: its due date, the total amount borrowed, and whatever other information you think is necessary. That way, no arguments because of misinterpretation will come up later. With promissory notes, as with other contracts, however, states differ in their requirements.

## *A contract is for you, not against you

Contracts clarify the when, where, and how of your goals. You and your contracting partner have the right to okay the conditions you include. Each of you can actively participate in creating your commitments.

A promissory note is a simple example of the support contracts offer. It documents the transaction and records the obligations the lender and borrower agree to. Besides the dollar figure of the loan and the repayment schedule, it can include some protection in advance for both contractors. For instance, you might want to establish a procedure that would be followed if one of you dies. The promissory note serves as a memory jogger. There is an added benefit; by sealing your exchange in a contract that follows the rules, your agreement is backed by law.

### *Aren't contracts primarily for big deals?

What do lovers have in common with Chrysler Corporation and the United Auto Workers Union? Professor Marjorie Shultz points out, "Even hard-core commercial contracts include many of the issues and elements that relationship contracts do: emotions, long duration, hard-to-predict changes over time, the need to adjust and accommodate, and expectations that are not fully articulated."

### *What are the rules?*

We use legal agreements to support what we want to accomplish. However, if we don't follow the guidelines required by Contract Law, we defeat our purposes. Whether contracts are simple or complex, written by hand while leaning on the back of a truck or devised by a staff of attorneys, there are basic standards that must be met for them to be legally enforceable.

### *No contract that supports an illegal or immoral purpose, or otherwise goes against public policy, will be upheld by law

Public policy encompasses matters that affect the general public or the state. Illegal acts go against state laws; acts judged immoral go against law and conflict with social behavior rules. "In the Highwayman Case decided in 1725, a highway robber sued a fellow robber for failure to account for 'partnership profits.'"[2] The court found ". . . compelling public policy reasons to deny enforcement."[3] Having a contract does not guarantee that the court will enforce it. Your contract's promises must not conflict with the state's interests.

Public policy governs prenuptial agreements too. For example, courts have the final say in determining adequate child support in case of divorce even if couples have agreed on how they want to provide for their children. Public policy comes into play because children cannot defend themselves so the court must, and because the state does not want to become burdened. For any clause in a contract to be enforceable by law, it must not violate public policy.

## *The terms used in your contract must be clearly expressed

If the terms of your agreement are ambiguous, misinterpretation may cause problems. It is to your benefit to have a clearly written contract.

## *Hey, play fair!

If the contract you agree to is unfair to one of the contractors, it may not be enforced. "The question of fairness to a bargain is frequently a relevant issue when a party asserts a defense of capacity, undue influence, duress, mistake or misrepresentation."[4]

Brian handed Sharon a premarital contract the Monday before their wedding. He told her that she must sign or the wedding is off. Shocked, Sharon read the contract. She didn't like what it said, or how he gave it to her. What would you do if your lover handed you a prenuptial agreement at the last moment? Most of

---

2. Professors of Law Gordon D. Schaber and Claude D. Rohwer; *Contracts In A Nutshell*; West Publishing Co.; St. Paul; 1990; Section 120, "Public Policy or Illegality as a Defense"; p. 232.

3. Ibid., p. 232.

4. Ibid.; Section 119, "Unconscionability as a Defense; Procedural and Substantive"; p. 227.

the women I tell this story to worry, "Oh my god, a week before the wedding! She can't cancel, all the relatives are coming. What about the presents?" Men hearing the same story typically announce, "I'd walk. That means trouble." Both genders wonder what kind of communication Sharon and Brian could possibly have had.

Many premarital couples deal with their scary issues by avoiding them. Certainly Sharon and Brian did. But the week-before-the-wedding panic often brings out intense stuff. Lovers' doubts and fears come to the surface and explode in crazy ways. Fortunately, Sharon was able to express her reservations to Brian; plus she had a friend who was a lawyer. He worked fast to make changes in Brian's proposed premarital contract that were satisfactory to Sharon. The wedding went as planned, but Sharon and Brian still had a lot of communication work ahead. Contract Law recognizes that not all of us can react under duress as well as Sharon did.

As well, when a contractor is in a "weakened state of mind [that] can result from illness, advanced age, immaturity of youth, recent death of a spouse, use of alcohol or drugs, or any other circumstances that tend to deprive a person of the ability to make sound decisions,"[5] an undue influence defense may break the contract. If the contract is obviously weighted to one contractor's advantage at the other's expense, it may be considered unfair. Attorney Elias advises, "Just keep in mind that the best contracts benefit both parties more or less equally, . . ."[6] Don't commit to anything you don't want to do; promises are not taken lightly by Contract Law.

## What does it take to make a binding contract?

In order to have the law support your contract, there are certain criteria you and your contract-partner must meet.

---

5. Ibid.; Section 104, "Undue Influence"; p. 195.
6. Elias; *Make Your Own Contract*; p. 1:2.

## *The contractors

Who can contract? First of all, contractors must be competent. One legal measurement of competency is age. Under most states' regulations, by age eighteen you can contract for yourself. You can make a will, commit to a marriage contract, and certainly, enter the military under contract with your government. The second gauge is mental capacity, "Such a measure of intelligence, understanding, memory, and judgment relative to the particular transaction (e.g., making of will) as will enable the person to understand the nature of his act."[7] And, although we know that there can be many emotional and psychological impulses whirling about while a couple is contracting, unless they are extreme, they don't have an impact on one's legal capacity to contract.

## *Mutual benefits in the contract

Usually when we agree to an offer it is because we are getting something in return. We pay money for a car because we will get the car. In legal terms, the "consideration" is what each contractor gets for whatever they agree to do. The car is the consideration for the purchaser, the payment is the consideration for the seller. Consideration "is the primary basis for promise enforcement in the common law system."[8]

## *Mutual obligation and agreement in the contract

When we engage in a simple contract, such as the one Bob and I agreed to honor with Ned, we incorporate the same features that *Black's Law Dictionary* lists as two essentials of a lawful contract: "mutuality of agreement and mutuality of obligation." But after all,

---

7. Henry Campbell Black, M.A.; *Black's Law Dictionary*; Abridged Fifth Edition; West Publishing Co.; St. Paul; 1983; p. 510.
8. Schaber; *Contracts In A Nutshell*; Section 46, "Introduction to Consideration"; p. 75.

why else do we contract if not because each of us wants the transaction and we are willing to oblige ourselves in return. When Bob, Ned, and I signed our homemade contract, our signatures indicated that we agreed to its obligations.

## *Do you have confidence in your co-contractor?*

When you sign up to take dance lessons you expect that the description of what the lessons will cover, the number of sessions offered, and the representations of the teacher are all true. If not, you want your money back. In a legal contract as well, you presume that what the other contractor agrees to, he will do. When we develop our premarital contract, we expect that our mate is bargaining in good faith, not trying to take advantage of us or the situation. Good faith bargaining is not only the basis for mutual trust, but without it your contract can be in trouble. The contractual requirement of good faith bargaining may well require that premarital contractors disclose their assets and debts to each other. Full financial disclosure shows that you are not trying to defraud one another by holding back any information.

## *What makes a contract a contract?*

A contract has three parts: the beginning—where background details are included; the middle—where your promises are; and the end— where the contractors sign. A common credit card agreement and Diane and Jake's prenuptial agreement illustrate the basic parts of a contract.

## *The Beginning*

This section contains pertinent information for anyone who reads the contract. For example, in its beginning, an agreement I recently entered when I accepted a new credit card identifies that it is a Retail

Installment Credit Agreement between the bank and myself. It tells me when I can start using the charge card. In the introduction of their premarital agreement, Diane and Jake, avid premarital contractors met in the chapter "In This Troth Do We Pledge?", declare that their contract becomes effective "as of the date the marriage is solemnized." To establish their goal of having an intimate contract, Diane and Jake, besides stating their full names, also indicate that they will be referred to by their first names.

◀ PLEASE NOTE: Diane and Jake have generously allowed me to use their prenuptial agreement to illustrate clauses. Their prenuptial agreement fits their needs and their state's requirements. It is an example; in no way do I suggest that their agreement is appropriate or valid for you. For their complete agreement, see Appendix A.

## *In the beginning: Announcements

The first section in a premarital contract is called the "Recital." In the recital you declare your purposes and intentions: when you plan to marry and why you are entering into the prenuptial agreement. There are also other facts to announce, such as any prior marriages and children of those unions. Unusual circumstances that you want known, such as inheritances you expect in the future, can be declared here too. Diane and Jake proclaimed their intention to transfer her home to their joint ownership in their recital.

Bob and I used our recital to express our dreams and our goals. In fact, it was the writing of this portion of our premarital agreement that sustained us while we struggled through the difficult issues we had to confront. During the course of our premarital contracting, we were lucky to have the support and input of an attorney friend from another state. She was our sounding board, giving us her legal perspective while softening the harshness of the sample contracts we used for guides. As our completion deadline closed in on us, our calls to her increased from weekly to almost daily events.

One of those calls really upset Bob and me. Our lawyer friend suggested strongly that we take out all reference to our future dreams. Her concern was that it might cast doubt on the validity of our whole agreement if we didn't follow through on any one of our plans. Her suggestion brought me to tears. These dreams were our post-ARP declarations of our love and life together. But we followed her advice. Bob and I kept our declarations though, and we enjoy reading them and refining them at our anniversary celebrations. Perhaps we were too specific in our declarations for our future. Attorney Trine Bech thinks that it is appropriate to include in your recital, "general expectations that you are looking forward to without predicting your future."

Certainly, the process of developing your recital will help you and your partner crystallize your positions. Additionally, should enforcement ever become necessary, the information in the recital gives the court knowledge of your intent. You do not bind yourself legally to statements in this section. It is the location for relevant information— who the contractors are, and why and what they are contracting for.

## *"Therefore" clause

The "Therefore" clause announces your consideration and links your beginning declarations with the promises you and your contract-mate are about to make in the middle section of your contract.

NOW THEREFORE, in consideration of the mutual promises herein contained and the marriage about to be solemnized, the parties mutually covenant and agree as follows:[9]

---

9. Alexander Lindey and Louis I. Parley; *Lindey On Separation Agreements and Antenuptial Contracts*; Volume 3; Louis I. Parley, Esq., and Sarah D. Eldrich, Esq.; April 1992 Cumulative Supplement; Form 90.07 "Consideration: 'Therefore Clause.'"

## The Middle

The middle section is where it all happens. Here are the clauses that enumerate, often at great length and with convoluted detail, what you the contractors agree to do.

### *The middle: Clauses that state the specific goals of your contract

In this part of my charge card agreement there are numerous clauses that describe how the bank and I agree to perform. There is a clause that says that I am responsible for lost or stolen cards, and of course, another one informs me that I must pay any bills I accrue. There are clauses that outline when and how I must pay for the bank's service, as well as those that describe what the bank will do in return. Detailed explanations of what will happen if I don't pay my bills on time make up the bulk of this agreement. Premarital agreement clauses can cover property, income, children, an estate, and more. Clauses unique to prenuptial agreements will be discussed at length in the following chapter.

### *The middle: You-look-familiar clauses

My credit card agreement and Diane and Jake's prenuptial agreement have similar safeguard clauses. Although they may be written somewhat differently, they prevent certain common, contractual points from becoming problems. Most contracts have the following clauses:

*Familiar Face #1: Law Applicable clause.* My credit card contract announces that the laws of the state the bank is located in and Federal Laws and Regulations rule. Bob's and my premarital agreement also states which law applies. Since we were married in New Mexico and planned to live in New Jersey only for a year before relocating, we needed to establish which state's laws ruled for our premarital agreement. Our clause was direct:

◀ SITUS: The laws of the State of New Jersey shall govern the execution and enforcement of this Agreement.

Even with this clause, there is no guarantee that the state you move to will indeed follow your prior state's rules, or interpret similarly worded regulations the same way. If you plan to move to another state, it is important to speak with an attorney familiar with that state's law.

*Familiar Face #2: Non-waiver clause.* Called by my credit card application the "Delay in Enforcement" clause, it is there to make sure that the bank does not lose any of its rights if they do not enforce them right away. The text in Diane and Jake's premarital contract is:

◀ The failure of either of us to insist upon strict performance of any of the provisions of this Agreement shall not be deemed a waiver of any subsequent breach of default of any provision contained in this Agreement.[10]

In real life, we don't often do exactly as we agree to do. Day-to-day actions and decisions happen so fast that sometimes it is too cumbersome to keep to the letter of our premarital contract's arrangements. We may commingle our incomes, or use one individual's asset for joint reasons even though we had agreed not to do that in our prenuptial agreement. This clause keeps our goals in mind, even if we don't always.

*Familiar Face #3: Survivorship clause.* A real estate contract's survivorship clause binds the contract to sellers' and buyers' heirs, successors, and assigns. My credit card application made no mention of successors' responsibilities or rights. In our premarital contract, Bob and I went into great detail about how we wanted our separate

---

10. Diane and Jake's Premarital Agreement; Clause 12.5., "Modification or Waiver."

and joint properties passed along to our heirs. The survivorship statement we used to cement our details, however, was quite simple:

◀ This Agreement shall inure to the benefit of each of us and our heirs.

*Familiar Face #4: Entire Agreement clause.* The Entire Agreement clause states that the contract supersedes all prior agreements, written or oral, and often goes on to verify that there are no other agreements.

◀ This Agreement contains the entire understanding between us. There are no representations, warranties, promises, covenants, or understandings, oral or otherwise, direct or indirect, implicit or implied, other than those expressly set forth herein.[11]

If this last clause motivates you to demand that your lawyer use simple sentences in your contract, good! But do keep in mind that your attorney, in your best interest, is satisfying legal requirements that you may not be aware exist.

*Familiar Face #5: Amendment clause.* Sometimes called the "Modification" clause, it will generally require that any amendments to the contract be in writing and be signed by both contractors—in the case of a real estate contract, for example, the buyer and the seller, and for a prenuptial agreement, you and your lover. The *Uniform Premarital Agreement Act*[12] suggests in its Section 5, "Amendment, Revocation," that "After marriage, a premarital agreement may be amended or revoked only by a written agreement signed by the parties. The amended agreement or the revocation is enforceable without consideration." Not all states, though, have adopted the *Uniform Premarital Agreement Act,* so it is important to verify your state's amendment qualifications with your attorney.

In case you do want to amend your premarital contract, be sure

---

11. Diane and Jake's Agreement; Clause 11.4., "Entire Agreement."
12. In 1983 the National Conference of Commissioners on Uniform State Laws drafted the *Uniform Premarital Agreement Act.* It was approved by the American Bar Association on February 13, 1984.

you specifically refer to what you are revising, and, if they are relevant, update your financial disclosure exhibits.

***Familiar Face #6: Revocation clause.*** The "Termination" clause in a sample Prenuptial Agreement prepared by Attorney George F. Bearup states:

◀ HUSBAND and WIFE may terminate this Agreement only by a written document, dated, witnessed and signed by both. It shall automatically terminate upon the deaths of both HUSBAND and WIFE, unless sooner revoked under the specific terms of this Agreement.[13]

There is no set time limit for your premarital contract; it is up to you and your requirements. Burt felt his fears would be dispelled if his and Rita's marriage lasted for a long time, so they agreed that their prenuptial agreement would self-destruct in ten years. Certain goals fade with the assurances of time and experience; others are relevant forever. Bob and I planned to keep our contract valid until one of us died because of the clauses pertaining to our children and stepchildren.

***Familiar Face #7: Severability clause.*** Other times called the "Saving clause," "Separability clause," or "Partial Invalidity clause," the "Severability clause" states that if one clause in the contract is invalid, the remaining clauses are still in effect.

◀ Should any provisions of this Agreement be held invalid or unenforceable by any court of competent jurisdiction, all other provisions shall, nonetheless, continue in full force and effect, to the extent that the remaining provisions are fair, just and equitable.[14]

*Familiar faces make new circumstances less scary. Your premarital contract is just like other contracts.*

---

13. George F. Bearup, Esq.; "Prenuptial Agreements: A Time for a Change in Public Policy"; *Michigan Bar Journal*; October 1989; Sample Prenuptial Agreement, Clause 16, "Termination"; p. 992.

14. Diane and Jake's Premarital Agreement; Clause 12.4., "Severability."

## *What do you mean by that?*

Some of your contractual terms may need to be defined. My charge card contract defined what the bank means by "Holder" of the card. Not only me, but anyone else I allow to use the card is a "holder." In our premarital agreement, Bob and I identified what measurement we would use for our children's "emancipation"—their coming of age. That is not a simple decision, but one that can be encumbered by all sorts of emotions. When will your children be independent? At eighteen, whenever they graduate college, age twenty-one, or not until they complete their doctoral thesis? In their contract, Diane and Jake defined what they meant by termination of marriage. Have you and your mate defined "ownership" of your property yet?

## *Hey, that's mine . . . uh, whose is it?*

Deciding who will own what is not as simple as you may think. Ownership is not just a word, nor is it merely a perception. Decisions of which is whose may hinge on your philosophy of life. While you are single, your property—possessions, real estate property, or other assets—is clearly yours. Once you move in with someone, cohabit with a mate, or get married ownership lines are arbitrarily apportioned by your state—unless you define your own. Contracts that deal with such items as your marital home or other assets have to make clear who owns what. Do you own the property, or do you and your partner own it? If both of you own it, how?

## *Ours

Okay, you and your mate have decided that you will own the property jointly. You are still not relieved from making further decisions. How do you want to share that possession? It is important to know the ownership options and property rules of your state so that you and your mate can use your prenuptial agreement to keep your property boundaries where you want them to be.

## *This is mine, this is yours, but this is ours

People can own real estate jointly in various ways. The current styles available to select from are tenants in common, joint tenants, and tenants by the entirety. These are undivided interest ownerships. "Each tenant has an equal right to make use of and enjoy the entire property."[15] You and your mate do not have to own equal shares of a particular property. For example, if one partner only owns a quarter interest ". . . the holder is entitled to one-quarter of all profits and sale proceeds but has a right to possession of the whole."[16] You and your mate can arrange the ownership of your different properties in various ways.

### *Tenants in common*

With this form of joint ownership, each owner has an interest in the property. If one dies, his share goes to his heirs, not to the other property owner. If he wants to, an individual owner can sell his share to anyone else.

### *Joint tenancy*

Joint tenancy has the right of survivorship. Each owner owns part interest in the entire property. One owner may sell her share but if one of you dies, the other one retains the whole property.

### *Tenancy by the entirety*

This ownership, like joint tenancy, has the right of survivorship, but it is limited to husbands and wives. Neither spouse may sell his share

---

15. Steven H. Gifis; *Barron's Law Dictionary*, Second Edition; Barron's Educational Series, Inc.; New York; 1984; p. 496.
16. Ibid.; p. 497.

of the property without the other spouse's consent. If one of you dies, the other spouse owns the whole property to the exclusion of the first spouse's heirs.

Professor Nadine Taub advises, "It is crucial to know as much as you can about the law regarding property arrangements and enforceability in the particular jurisdiction you are likely to be in and to be very aware not just of the abstract legal principles, but in fact what the judicial practice is." Only then can you and your mate define what you mean by ownership and identify what you want.

### That's all folks: The End

The middle portion of your contract is the most exhausting part of the three to complete. Be thankful for endings.

### *It's a done deal

The conclusion of the contract is where we physically show our agreement. The various forms of contracts between individuals have different requirements to seal the bargain—to execute the contract. My Retail Installment Agreement does not have a formal signature page. I will indicate that I agree to the contract's clauses when I use the card for the first time. The bank shows its agreement when it pays my first charge. In some states, a real estate Purchase and Sale Agreement not only requires the buyer's and seller's signatures, but the signatures of the selling and listing agents as well.

Your state may require that prenuptial agreements be witnessed and notarized. Notaries and witnesses do not read your contract. All they do is corroborate that you, the signer, are who you say you are. Generally, if you are not personally known to the notary, your driver's license and one of your charge cards or a bank account passbook are all that you need to identify yourself. More than witnessing, your state may require an acknowledgment. To acknowledge your contract you attest to a notary that you are signing the contract willingly and that you swear its contents are true. The notary public is authorized by his state to take your oath which he then certifies with his official seal. See the execution page of Diane and Jake's contract for an example of an acknowledgment. Usually, notaries can be found at banks, drug stores, real estate offices, title companies, or law offices. Generally, they don't charge for their services, or, they ask a nominal fee.

## *Recording your contract

Some states also "provide for the recording of agreements on the land records."[17] Find out from your attorney whether that is required by your state. Transfer of real property may need some auxiliary action. Jake and Diane solidified their declared transfer of home ownership by executing, once they were married, a deed of joint ownership. Deeds must be recorded.

### *Self-protection is the best insurance*

There are certain interactions that we engage in where we don't think twice about our commitments because they won't cost us too much in money, time, effort, or emotion. But when you are contracting for something that is important to you, it is best to put your agreement in some form of writing. Sam Goldwyn reportedly said, "A verbal contract isn't worth the paper it's written on." Friends, relatives, or business connections are better protected by written contracts. The least that a contract avoids is hard feelings based on misunderstandings. The most that the process of writing your agreement accomplishes is that it makes you and your contracting partner focus on what you agree to live by. Mutual protection motivates both of you to design the best agreement possible.

---

17. Parley; *Lindey On Separation Agreements and Antenuptial Contracts*; Chapter 90; Section 90.05 D., "Recording."

## *Practical tips*

Whether you or your attorney prepares your contract there are some helpful pointers to keep in mind:

*Tip #1:* Make sure you execute enough original documents so that you, your mate, and your attorneys each have one. An original is the document you actually sign. Photocopies are good to keep as extras, but they are not originals.

*Tip #2:* Once the original premarital contracts have been stapled—and that ought to happen before you sign—do not remove the staples. This way it is clear that no page has been added or removed. Some attorneys advise signers to initial each page of the contract.

*Tip #3:* Before you sign the document, reread it. Typographical errors can alter your intended meaning. People overlook, leave out, or add words that might change what your intentions are. Also, assuring yourself once again that everything you worried about has been covered will make the contract easier to sign.

*Tip #4:* Changes can be handwritten into the contract. Don't fret, the prenuptial agreement does not have to be reprinted. But initial each change so that it is certain that you have okayed them.

*Tip #5:* If your contract has to be witnessed or notarized, don't sign it ahead of time.

**Execute your contract before you marry.**

## *Do I really have to do what I agree to do?*

The strength of your contract is your contract-mate's and your honor. Most of us sign a contract expecting to fulfill our obligations. The motivation driving us is what we are gaining from the contractual agreement. Professor Shultz says, "It is true that in contracts in general, enforcement is only an issue in a tiny fraction of cases. In the first place it is only an issue where a dispute arises. The majority of contracts will be performed and they will be honored, or they will be mutually adjusted in a way that both parties agree to."

### Unspoken marriage contract alert

When you sign most contracts, you have a document that tells you what you have agreed to do and what the results will be. But, the " 'marriage contract' [between the marital couple and the state] is unlike most contracts: its provisions are unwritten, its penalties are unspecified, and the terms of the contract are typically unknown to the contracting parties."[18] Additionally, to know the conditions your state puts on your marriage you have to search for them. To inform your mate and the state of the terms you want in your marriage, you have to enter into a legally binding prenuptial agreement.

### Where do we begin talking this time?
Your *whys* make your lover wise!

- Does premarital contracting with your lover scare you?
- Are you fair to your mate?
- Are you fair to yourself?
- Do you want a premarital contract?

### Discussion starter:

- What marriage vows do you want to pledge to in your wedding ceremony?

---

18. Lenore J. Weitzman; *The Marriage Contract: Spouses, Lovers, and the Law*; The Free Press, a Division of Macmillan Publishing Co, Inc.; New York; 1983; p. xv.

For those of you who would like to do some additional reading on the subject of this chapter:

*Contracts In a Nut Shell*, Gordon D. Schaber and Claude D. Rohwer, Professors of Law
*Don't Get Married Until You Read This: A Layman's Guide to Prenuptial Agreements*, David Saltman and Harry Schaffner
*Family Law In a Nut Shell*, Harry D. Krause, Professor of Law
*Make Your Own Contract: Simple Contracts For Personal Use*, Stephen Elias

There are books available in local bookstores and libraries that cover specific states' Family Law.

# 10 *Your Premarital Agreement*

*Prepare a partnership covenant.*

> The highest compact we can make with our fellow is—"Let there be truth between us two forevermore."
>
> RALPH WALDO EMERSON

Can you tell your mate what you are most afraid will happen if you marry?

Would you tie the knot with unspoken and unresolved issues remaining between you and your partner?

Do you want to determine the structure of your marriage?

"I AM AFRAID to marry. It's a trap," says Carla. She explains why. "I know Tony loves me and I love him, but I'm still afraid that I will lose too much of what is important to me if we marry." Carla is not unique in her feelings. Although in the not very distant past women focused on getting married and men strove to stay single, now many women resist marriage too. Lovers fear such a commitment may damage their future goals and past achievements.

Partners who are contemplating marriage, in trepidation or with confidence, have two options for dealing with their personal concerns. You can determine what goes into your marriage contract and prevent traps, or you can accept what others have ordered. If you do not have a prenuptial agreement, or if you have one that does not include elements that are important to you, the laws of your state govern your marriage. If you have gotten anything out of this book, I hope it is that premarital contracts do not have to be divorce-decrees-in-advance. Instead, they can be the outcome of a couple's loving search for how they want their partnership to function. Are you ready to commit to your personalized marital structure?

## *Legal advice*

The goal of this chapter is to inspire your premarital contracting. A reminder: it is necessary for you to call on your own legal counsel to make sure that your prenuptial agreement will accomplish what you want. This book, the *Uniform Premarital Agreement Act,* and Jake and Diane's example in no way purports to fill that need. Don't forget that each state has different laws and regulations. Thus, your friend's antenuptial[1] agreement, or a sample clause found in Diane and Jake's contract, in this book, or from any other source may not satisfy your state's requirements or address your unique specifics. This chapter offers a buffet of information, but you are in charge of the whole meal.

## *Lovers' input

Although there are lawyers capable of guiding you through the legal requirements of your contract, very few can give you guidance on how to communicate with your lover, how to contract together, and what topics you both want to include in your covenant. That is your work.

---

1. "Antenuptial," interchangeable with "prenuptial," means "Made or done before a marriage." Black; *Black's Law Dictionary*; p. 48.

## *Whether or not you are married, commitments are made

"Every relationship entered into with any expectation of permanence, however, creates some legal and moral obligations."[2] Since states' laws have regulations that impact cohabitation as well as marriage, lovers who live together unmarried would be wise to establish what they agree to honor. Although this chapter focuses on prenuptial agreements, couples interested in cohabitation contracts will find relevant material as well.

### *It's okay to contract!*

The **Uniform Premarital Agreement Act** defines a premarital agreement as "an agreement between prospective spouses made in contemplation of marriage and to be effective upon marriage." That's all it is; not painful, not horrendous, just an agreement. *Lindey On Separation Agreements and Antenuptial Contracts,* a reference source that lawyers use for information on legal forms, states, "As a consequence of either common law or statute, all fifty states and the District of Columbia will recognize and enforce a validly made premarital agreement."[3] Lovers, you do not have to be afraid of a prenuptial agreement. Partners, you are not wasting your time and effort. We can, and our states will, respect our prenuptial contracts.

### *What can go into a prenuptial agreement?*

The format of a prenuptial agreement basically parallels other contractual forms. Still, the topics are different. The purpose of many clauses that my lawyer and Bob's added became clear to us as we became more familiar with Contract Law requirements, but our final

---

2. American Bar Association; *Your Legal Guide To Marriage—and Other Relationships*; p. 11.

3. Cumulative Supplement to *Lindey On Separation Agreements and Antenuptial Contracts*; Revised Edition; 1989 Supplement by Louis I. Parley, Esq., and Sarah D. Eldrich, Esq.; Volume 3; Matthew Bender; October 1989; Section 90.02, p. 90-28 to p. 90-32.

premarital agreement did not stray far from our original premarital contracting lists.

TOPICS IN BOB AND JACQUELINE'S
PRENUPTIAL AGREEMENT:

The effective date of our agreement is the date we marry. Our names.

Recitals: our history and our intentions

"Now, therefore" clause: our consideration is our marriage and our promises to each other set forth below:

A. We confirm our statements in our Recitals
B. Premarital property
    1. Separate
    2. Joint
C. Property acquired during the marriage
    1. Separate
    2. Marital
D. Premarital debts
    1. How they will be paid off
E. Our incomes
    1. Marital fund
    2. Separate
F. Our children
    1. Support
    2. Inheritances
G. In case we divorce
    1. We give up any claim to spousal support
    2. We waive our rights to each other's separate property
H. When we die
    1. We renounce inheritance rights under marital laws, except what we promise in this agreement
    2. Survivors: us and our heirs
I. This prenuptial agreement is in effect only if we marry
J. Disclosure: We are familiar with each other's finances and have seen one another's financial disclosure exhibits
    1. We will not ask for additional financial rights other than those included in this agreement

K. If needed, this Agreement shall be the basis for judgment regarding termination of marriage

L. To alter this agreement

    1. Changes must be in writing

M. If this agreement is not strictly enforced, it does not mean it isn't
in effect

N. House tidying clauses

    1. Our attorneys' names

    2. We prepared the agreement ourselves

    3. We will supply further documents if they are needed

    4. The laws of the state of New Jersey shall govern the exe-
cution and enforcement of this Agreement

O. Our financial exhibits

P. Execution page

    1. Our signatures and dates

    2. Notary acknowledgments and witnesses for each of us

Our categories may not suit your needs or be enough for your goals;
certainly, our details are ours alone. Any similarity of topics, though,
is due to the universality of prenuptial and marital issues.

## The parts of a prenuptial agreement

Diane and Jake's premarital contract format will be our guide.[4]
Clauses from other sources are offered as well to illustrate additional
needs of premarital couples. The headings for clauses come from
Diane and Jake's contract. They are not the only headings that can
be used, nor is their order the only way.

## *The Recital

This is the preamble to your contractual promises. As we reached
the point in our contracting when we had to make hard decisions,
Bob and I found that the fun we had writing our recital portion set

---

4. Diane and Jake's complete prenuptial agreement is in the Appendix.

a positive mood. So we started our initial contracting sessions writing out a special goal to put in our recitals; that encouraged us to grab our spades and dig into our emotionally challenging issues.

The recital is the place to include your reasons for contracting, your individual histories, and current information; things that are not legally binding. Diane and Jake explained themselves in their recital:

◄ A. We intend to marry on 27 August 1989, and have been living together since October 1988 at a house owned by Diane in Bidwell, North Carolina. Diane has two daughters, Susan and Tracy, by a prior marriage. Jake has one son, Bill, by a prior marriage. We each want to preserve our abilities to provide for our children. We desire to define our financial rights and responsibilities.

◄ B. Diane intends to make a transfer to Jake of a half interest in her Bidwell house, so that the marital home will be in both of our names as tenants by the entirety and to do this as a public symbol of our marriage.

The recital does not hold promises; instead, it states your intentions. Diane and Jake included statements about expected future inheritances and acknowledged that each of them was familiar with the other's financial circumstances. Two other important intentions were referred to as well: provisions regarding support in the event of the dissolution of their marriage, and waivers of certain survivors' rights in case of death. Some couples' recitals also indicate how they were represented by attorneys.[5]

Lawyers give varied recommendations as to what premarital contractors ought to put into recitals. Their advice runs the gamut from such suggestions as, "Lovers ought to put in a complete background for the arrangements they have in their premarital contract," to, "Don't put in any goals because if they aren't fulfilled they may nullify the contract." If you do want to include plans or philosophical statements about your relationship, attorney M. Dee Samuels suggests specifying, "We don't intend these statements to be legally

---

5. See *Lindey On Separation Agreements and Antenuptial Contracts*; Recital clauses, Forms 90.01 through 90.06.

enforceable or affect the other part of our agreement. However, it is important for us to have a statement of our goals." The times and your state will influence what you choose to include in your recital as well as the many other decisions you will face while you develop your contract. Your lawyer can guide you.

One sample prenuptial agreement included an intriguing recital clause:

◀ HUSBAND and WIFE believe that it would be conducive to the harmony, success and strength of their anticipated marriage to incorporate their verbal prenuptial agreement into a written document so that they may devote their full attention to the success, growth and enjoyment of their marriage without anxiety concerning the efficacy or enforceability of their verbal agreement.[6]

***Therefore clause.*** The "Therefore" *clause* establishes the consideration for your prenuptial agreement. Consideration is what each contractor gives and receives.

◀ NOW THEREFORE, in consideration of the mutual promises hereinbelow set forth and our contemplated marriage, we hereto agree as follows:[7]

This clause leads into the legally binding promises of your prenuptial agreement.


## *Okay, it's off to the races*

In this chapter we will discuss a variety of clauses that illustrate the substance of a premarital contract. When you are ready, look over Diane and Jake's contract so that you can get the sense of a complete premarital agreement. Also, this would be a good time to locate a

---

6. George F. Bearup, Esq.; "Prenuptial Agreements: A Time for a Change in Public Policy"; *Michigan Bar Journal*; October 1989; Section N.; p. 989. This article offers a brief and interesting history of contemporary premarital contracts.

7. Diane and Jake's "Now Therefore" clause.

copy of *Lindey On Separation Agreements and Antenuptial Contracts*
for more clauses that you may want to use in your prenuptial agreement. Ask your lawyer where you can see the most recent edition;
perhaps she has a copy or can locate one for you. If not, find a library
that does. You will see how clauses are written, which ones may be
almost right for your needs. You will get additional ideas to discuss
with your mate, and then, with your attorney. Now, let's take a look
at clauses.

## *Property clauses*

What is property? As defined in the **Uniform Premarital
Agreement Act**, the word property "means an interest, present or
future, legal or equitable, vested or contingent, in real or personal
property, including income and earnings."[8] See the previous chapter
for a discussion on types of real estate property ownership. Prenuptial
agreement clauses that are pertinent to property issues are divided
into two categories: premarital ownership and property acquired during the marriage.

## *Premarital property clauses: Separate property

The first clause in this section will comprehensively define what you
and your mate mean by separate property, and how you each will
retain separate ownership of the so-described properties.[9] Both of
you can prepare financial statements to identify your separate assets.
These lists must be attached to your contract. Diane and Jake added
a separate property clause that explained the impending transfer of
the house title.
    *Lindey* includes a sample clause for a situation in which the home

8. *Uniform Premarital Agreement Act*; Section 1.(2) "Definitions."
9. See Diane and Jake's contract; section 3.1., "Separate Property," and *Lindey*; Form 90.10,
"Separate Assets."

is owned by one partner and joint or separate funds will most likely
be spent on the house for both partners' use:

◀ . . . the use of any joint funds, or of any separate funds contributed
by [the non-owner] . . . shall not create any interest in the property in
[the non-owner]. However, if joint funds are used to make any capital
improvements on the property . . . [the non-owner] shall thereafter
have a lien against the property to the extent of one half of the total
joint funds so used, or the full amount of the separate funds contributed, which lien shall be paid upon the sale of the property or the
termination of the parties' marriage, or the death of [the owner],
whichever shall first occur, . . . [10]

## *Premarital property clauses: Joint property

Some premarital partners meticulously plot their purchases of joint-
use items. One pays for the coffee grinder, the other pays for the can
opener; both items are for shared use, but they are not jointly owned.
That way, each is spending about the same amount of money, but
in case they split up, they know what is whose. Other couples mean
to keep strict boundaries, but sometimes both chip in on a purchase.
A clause stating how you want to deal with jointly owned property
would be in order here. [11]

## *Property acquired during the marriage clauses: Separate property

The goal of this section is to maintain your separate property boundaries while recognizing that the specific assets that make up your
separate property may change. One of *Lindey*'s examples states it
concisely:

---

10. *Lindey*; Form 90.14, "Sole Ownership of Residence; Effect of Joint Payments of
Expenses."

11. See Diane and Jake's solution in their premarital agreement, clause 3.3, "Joint Property."

◀ Any assets obtained by either party as a consequence of the use, investment, reinvestment or any transfer of any portion of his or her separate estate, and any income therefrom, and any appreciation in the value thereof, shall remain part of his or her separate estate.[12]

You and your lover are not the only ones looking at each other's contribution to your marriage. To perform its duty in determining a settlement, a divorce court will scrutinize how, in your prenuptial agreement, you assign ownership of income and assets gained during your marriage. Take a pension plan as an example. Courts may look at the pension plan you and your company set up years before you married "as with other property constituting the marital estate, the value of the pension interest must be included in the property division."[13] That is, unless you establish the apportionment of your property in your prenuptial agreement. How do you want to own your pension plan? Is it yours, or is it for you and your spouse? Do you want to clarify the ownership of other assets?

## *Property acquired during the marriage clauses: Marital property

What is separate property and what is joint property once we marry? Real estate and personal property that you and your mate obtain in joint name are joint assets. The title of your car can be in both names or in one partner's name; so can the ownership of your home. Unless you specify differently in your premarital agreement, your state's regulations determine how your marital property is treated. In Diane and Jake's contract, what they consider marital property is clearly identified, but they rely on three additional clauses to make their identification firm. Their lawyers wanted to make sure that there would be no misinterpretations.[14]

Property clauses can reveal how lovers view their partnership.

---

12. *Lindey*; Form 90.11, "Income from and Reinvestment of Separate Assets."

13. Steinke v. Steinke, 126 Wis.2d 372, 376 N.W.2d 839 (1985) quoted in 15 FLR 1441, Digest of Opinion for Rodak v. Rodak; Wis CtApp 2dDist. No. 88-1269; 4/12/89, released 6/28/89.

14. Diane and Jake's contract, Section 4, "Property Acquired During The Marriage."

Jane Bryant Quinn, a regular columnist for *Newsweek*, describes this scenario, "A homemaker, in a state without community property, feels uneasy about her position. She's not fretting about divorce, only about her utter dependency. A written property agreement makes it clear that she's a full partner in the marital enterprise."[15] The question remains as to what of yours you want to devote to your relationship, and what you want to keep for your individual goals. You don't have to give up control of your assets any more than you must relinquish your individual identity. But it requires a certain leap of faith, based on your evaluation of your lover and your relationship, to let go of the drive to stand guard. By committing yourselves to your partnership, you and your lover gain. It is self-defeating to give too much or too little. You decide the proportions.

## *Premarital Debts*

It is here in your contract that you and your mate state how you want to pay out the debts listed on your financial statements. You and your lover can only benefit by being clear to one another about your financial concerns and goals.

## *Dedication Of Each Of Our Incomes*

### *Separate income

We see in Diane and Jake's contract, section 4, *"Property Acquired During The Marriage,"* that you can make sure that income gained as a result of the sale or any change to your assets remains separate property. You can reaffirm that here. But there are other income arrangements to make clear as well. Do you and your mate intend to

15. Jane Bryant Quinn; "When The Pre-Nuptial Agreement Is Not Enough"; *The West Side Spirit*; New York; 2/13/90; p. 16.

commingle your salaries?[16] Or do you both agree to identify in great detail who pays for what so that you do not mix your incomes together? It is up to you and your mate to decide how your incomes, your property, and your marriage operate. Is it a partnership, or not? How much of a partnership is it? Everything equal, or equitable? Are your interests being respected by you as much as your mate does hers? Even if you choose to keep your incomes separate, there are ways to work together so that you cement your partnership, not divide it.

## *Marital fund partnership

> Jan operates her child-care business at home. Although she works long hours, she earns less than her husband Craig does. Nevertheless, because their two toddlers participate in Jan's program, they don't incur child-care costs. The question—how to handle their individual incomes?—needed their answer. Jan and Craig agreed to have a joint marital fund. Craig contributes more money because he earns more. They each feel that arrangement is fair because they value Jan's care of their children. They have equal responsibility and control of their joint fund.

There are all sorts of economic configurations. Both partners earn similar salaries; one mate doesn't earn income, but maintains the home; elderly premarital lovers want to protect the bulk of their individual estates for their respective heirs, but have retirement income to share; or young lovers who are starting out with small earning power are but a few. Each couple has the opportunity to design a partnership relationship that uses some kind of joint fund. The authors of *Don't Get Married Until You Read This* suggest a way to create a marital property fund:

◀ During the course of the marriage the Parties shall make equal [or whatever increment you choose] periodic contributions to a fund for

---

16. *Lindey's* Form 90.15 offers one way to address the "Consequences of Commingling Income and Assets." See clause on following page.

the maintenance of their household and the care and support of the children of the marriage. All property purchased with the proceeds of this fund shall be deemed marital property. Each party shall have equal rights in regard to the management of and disposition of all marital property.[17]

If you do create a marital fund, you also can determine what happens to its contents if your marriage ends because of divorce or death. Allen and Cindy, encountered in the chapter "What's There to Talk About?" decided that, although Allen put in more money, their joint fund would be split down the middle if they divorced. They also agreed that if one of them died their fund went the way of their other joint property, to the survivor. Many partners are concerned that their commingling of funds not be construed to mean that they agree to give up their separate assets to joint ownership. *Lindey's* "Consequences of Commingling Income and Assets," Form 90.15, addresses that concern:

◀ . . . It is the parties' intention that such commingling or pooling of assets not be interpreted to imply any abandonment of the terms and provisions of this Agreement. . . .

*Lindey* points out that the filing of joint income tax returns does not connote abandonment of any of the terms set forth in the agreement. An outgrowth issue for some couples might be—if you file joint income tax returns will you prorate tax payments? If so, how?

## *Creativity and love inspire good ideas

Instead of writing a contract that is a who-pays-for-what down to the purchase of toothpaste, you can link your separate contributions. For example, mates could set up a joint checking account in which each deposits a percentage of their income based on earnings and contributions to the marital partnership. Lovers gain emotional sustenance

---

17. David Saltman, J.D., L.L.M. and Harry Schaffner, J.D.; *Don't Get Married Until You Read This: A Layman's Guide To Prenuptial Agreements*; Barron's; New York; 1989; Section 3.04, "Creation of Marital Property Fund"; p. 133.

from working together to build joint property. It is concrete testimony of their faith in their relationship.

## The state speaks

State law enters our private world of marriage at death and divorce, the very times when it is most difficult to face outside pressures. Why not establish ahead of time what you want to do in case of divorce or death and have it in place?

## Termination of marriage clauses

Including clauses that will be relevant only if your marriage dissolves because of divorce, does not mean that you want or expect your marriage to fail. But by discussing these issues during your premarital contracting you both can give your creative solutions the support of your love. "Today, it is fairly well established that courts will enforce certain kinds of provisions of premarital contracts dealing with divorce."[18] But the divorce court will check your provisions to make sure that they honor the necessary requirements. Fair warning: use attorneys knowledgeable in Family Law.

### Termination of marriage clauses help us realize how much we want to stay together

## Termination of marriage clauses: Children

Until we have children, most of us find it almost impossible to imagine what they or we, as parents, will be like. True, we do have values and philosophies that we expect to incorporate into our family dynamics, but until our kids arrive, we don't know anything for sure. Premarital contracting gives you and your mate the enjoyable oppor-

---

18. American Bar Association; *Your Legal Guide to Marriage*; p. 13.

tunity to talk about children. It is a serious subject as well. Although your experts can give you concrete ways to achieve your estate plan, satisfactory child support and custody arrangements to be followed in case you and your mate divorce are not so easily chosen.

## *Child support

*Your Legal Guide to Marriage* points out that "an agreement about child support is not enforceable if it adversely affects a child's right to parental support; it might be enforceable if it calls for more rather than less financial support than a court would award in the absence of an agreement."[19]

> Brandon is an electrician and Martha manages a local coffee shop. They have worked hard for years. They also work hard to make their relationship a success. Through their premarital contracting, Martha and Brandon have made it clear to each other that they will raise their children in partnership. They have also vowed to stay committed to their children even if their marriage breaks up. In their premarital agreement they promised that, in case of divorce, they would each contribute to their children's support. Also, if they disagreed on any big expenses for their children, they agreed to go through a mediation process.

## *Child custody

> Martha and Brandon also outlined in their prenuptial agreement how they would care for their children. Since they believe that both the mother and the father are important, they promised that if they ever divorced, they'd alternate living with and caring for the children on a monthly basis.

> The Amended Divorce Law Of New York states that ". . . an

---

19. Ibid.; p. 15.

agreement between parties made before or during marriage is valid and enforceable in a matrimonial action. . . . and may include . . . 4) Provisions for the custody, education and maintenance of a child."[20] Your attorneys can guide you to the specifics of your state's requirements for child support and custody, once you have decided what you want to do.


## *Religious training

Children's religious upbringing frequently becomes an issue. Haden, one partner of the interfaith couple in the chapter "Isn't It Romantic?" did not discuss her worries with Mitch. Other couples do face religious training questions during their premarital contracting. Stating your intentions will definitely serve your marital happiness.


## *Stepchildren

Often, common parental concerns are compounded for stepfamilies. Not only must discipline values be established, but add to that chore the loaded psychological layers of stepfamilydom. How do we relate with each other's children? Must we support one another's children? Your attorneys can explain your legal responsibilities.


### *Termination of marriage clauses: Spouses*

Many couples have gone through divorces in which one or both spouses are bitter and spiteful. It would have been so much easier for the partners and their children if they could have separated in a kindly manner. Lovers can make some provisions now, just in case.

---

20. Amended Divorce Law of New York [L.1980, C.281; Domestic Relations Law Section 236, part B(3); quoted by George F. Bearup, Esq.; *Prenuptial Agreements: A Time for a Change in Public Policy*; p. 988.

## *Be giving, but not over generous

Lovers can include mutually beneficial provisions that encourage their marriage and as well define reasonable conditions that would take effect were their marriage to end in divorce. Be innovative. For example, asset questions are important for your marriage as well as in case of divorce. Attorney Gary Skoloff warns that problems arise down the road "if asset clauses are not fairly done because the have-not partner feels that the relationship is less than what they want concerning their rights and claims." One arrangement could be phased-in gifting to your mate in return for his waiving his spousal rights to your assets or your business.

As always, how lovers contract and the conditions they use to protect their interests reveal more than their economic requirements. Your choices can reflect your love and caring for each other, the domination of your fears over concern for your lover's comfort, or a mixture of many feelings.

## *Spousal maintenance clauses

Spousal support, as with child maintenance, can be included in your prenuptial agreements. "Now many states will enforce such provisions, although some still treat spousal support as beyond the power of spouses to control. . . . Courts may refuse to enforce provisions waiving support if enforcement would make a spouse eligible for welfare."[21]

The court will look at the circumstances of your marriage in reviewing your agreement. Its duration, the economic and non-economic contributions of each spouse, and the ability of the dependent spouse to support himself are factors judges use to make their decisions. You can have your say and be heard by the court if you include clear, fair clauses in your premarital agreement.

Since Diane and Jake are confident that they can take care of their individual economic comforts now and in the future, they waived

---

21. ABA; *Your Legal Guide to Marriage*; pp. 14–15.

their spousal support rights.[22] But many couples do not make their own decisions ahead of time and they must rely on court rulings. What about the partner who financially supports her mate through higher education and professional training? One court ruled that "A woman who made substantial contributions to the support of her husband both while he was in law school and while he was setting up his practice deserves more that the $5,400 lump sum alimony awarded her in their divorce decree. . . ."[23]

What about the spouse who gives up her career? Is she entitled to some economic security in case of divorce as well as in marriage? A court overturned an alimony award to the wife of a dentist for the amount of $169,000 to be paid over twenty years, saying that "we do not believe [the wife] is entitled to a financial windfall merely by virtue of the fact that she was married to [the husband] while he earned his degree. . . ."[24]

Some lawyers advise contracting couples to specifically acknowledge in their contracts the reasons why they have chosen a particular support or allocation arrangement. This is done to validate that the contract is fair and reasonable. A court will interpret a couple's contribution to their marriage by its standards. Making your intentions known expands the courts' view.

You can communicate important information about mutual promises regarding career moves, retirement plans, and anything else that you would like to prepare for. Now is the time; the place is in your premarital contract. Don't leave your arrangements to fate, estate laws, or a divorce court. After you and your mate clarify your goals, consult with your attorneys and research court rulings that have recently occurred in your state. It's up to the two of you to evaluate what kind of mutual support you want to give one another. But be fair or the court will have the final say.

22. Diane and Jake's agreement; clause 7.2., "Alimony, Maintenance or Support."

23. Robinson v. Irwin; Miss SupCt, No.58405, 6/21/89 reported in 15 F[amily] L[aw] R[eporter] 1433.

24. Krause v. Krause; Mich CtApp, No.100313; 5/15/89 reported in 15 FLR 1433.

# *Distribution of assets

After identifying their separate assets and stating the intended transfer of the marital house ownership, Diane and Jake reaffirmed that they waived their rights to each other's separate property.

◀ We specifically acknowledge and agree that in the event of the termination of the marriage, each of us waives any and all right we may have to any interest or claim to the separate property of the other, as hereinbefore defined, including right to future income from said separate property, including but not limited to dividends or rent.[25]

What may not be so easy is stating clearly how your joint property will be handled in case of divorce. Design your own solutions with the guidance of your attorneys. Remember also that there are other experts who can advise you.

# *Kettubahs need marital termination clauses too

Attorney Mel Frumkes[26] points out that "for an orthodox or a conservative Jewish wife, unless there is a 'get' (a religious bill of divorcement[27]), she is not divorced in the eyes of the rabbinate." The New York Board of Rabbis "recommended that all rabbis urge couples to sign prenuptial agreements, saying that in event of civil divorce, both partners will cooperate in arranging for a 'get.'"[28]

---

25. Diane and Jake's Agreement; clause 7.3., "Effect Upon Separate Property."
26. Melvyn B. Frumkes, Esq., principal of Frumkes and Associates, PA, practices Marital and Family Law in Miami, Florida.
27. George W. Cornell, Associated Press; "Jewish law leaves divorcees trapped in a marital limbo"; *The Miami Herald*; Friday, February 26, 1988.
28. Ibid.

*Legal what-ifs*


## *What if the validity of your prenuptial agreement is tested?

You want to make sure that your contract will be upheld. As we discussed in the prior chapter, Contract Law has established basic criteria to determine the validity of contracts. The criteria for premarital contracts have been refined to fit the occasion. The fact that prenuptial agreements will be scrutinized for unfair arrangements cannot be stressed too much. You and your lover may want to be fair for love's sake, but also, you must be fair to satisfy the court. To confuse the measure of unconscionability further, fairness of a premarital contract may be judged differently by individual states. For example, some states require that the substantive terms of your contract be fair only at the time of its execution, others measure fairness by the conditions at the time of enforcement too. What does your state use as its measurement of fair and reasonable terms for prenuptial agreements?


## *What if you move to a different state?

Bob and I moved to another state a year after we were married. Once we had settled into our new hometown, we contacted an attorney who specialized in Family Law and estate planning. Not only did we want to make sure that our New Jersey agreement was valid in our new state, but also we had some changes, raised by new circumstances, that we planned to attach to our contract. Because of Washington state law, to be sure our goals would be achieved we executed a new agreement. Though Bob and I knew in general what we wanted to do and we had already successfully completed a prenuptial agreement, we were both surprised that, again, it was difficult to choose the ways we wanted to accomplish our goals. Death and property issues definitely stimulate emotions.

# *What if you go to court?

Attorney Patricia Barr[29] alerts her clients, "If your contract's purpose is in part to protect the wife, it is important for you to know what a typical court judgment or settlement includes before you enter into your agreement and take that under advisement." Your local branch of the National Organization of Women is a good source for information. Courts' attitudes vary in states and districts, but gender bias is still a pervasive issue. "A quarter of the attorneys surveyed by the Washington State Task Force on Gender and Justice in the Courts said they believe women witnesses and litigants are regarded as less credible simply because they are female. . . . The task force found bias to be subtle and more a problem of individuals than the system. However, it said it still affects decisions in cases of divorce, sexual assault and domestic violence."[30] Gender bias can be thwarted by fair and concise premarital agreements.

# *What if you die?

Many couples who want to marry either hesitate or don't marry because they worry that their offspring of prior marriages may lose their inheritance. New innkeepers Marian and Dave, worried about their respective grandchildren, avoided marriage for a long time until their joint business venture forced them to seek answers. Using a prenuptial agreement, Dave and Marian contracted to protect each other's heirs by waiving their spousal inheritance rights. "The probate code, which, the court said, is declarative of public policy on the rights of omitted heirs, requires a written waiver, in 'clear and unmistakable' language, to defeat an omitted surviving spouse's right to inherit."[31]

---

29. Patricia Barr is on the Vermont Task Force on Gender Bias in the Legal System. It is a joint project of the Vermont Supreme Court and the Vermont Bar Association.

30. Associated Press; "Women are treated differently in court, many attorneys say"; *The Seattle Times/Seattle Post-Intelligencer*; Sunday, August 20, 1989.

31. Digest of Opinion 15 FLR 1031; In re Estate of Butler (Butler v. Stallcup); Calif CtApp2d Dist, No. BO30037, 10/20/88.

You don't have to waive your rights to everything. One affluent spouse devised a settlement for his less prosperous partner that made both of them happy. The wealthy partner proposed to the less wealthy one, "You get the house if I die before you, but when you die, the house will go to my kids." Everyone benefited, and all were comfortable enough with the arrangement.

### Legal Housekeeping

Your lawyer will suggest such housekeeping clauses to include in your prenuptial agreement as the "Consideration for Agreement," "Voluntary Execution," "Non-collusive Agreement," "Independent Counsel," and "Further Documents." The familiar face clauses discussed in the previous chapter will also be addressed by your attorney. And, you will find these clauses in Diane and Jake's prenuptial agreement.

### Where is matrimonial law heading?

Family Law is much more open to recognizing different marriage arrangements than in the past. Succinct and fair prenuptial agreements may broaden the law further. Issues that premarital contractors settle, if not now legally binding may be valid later.

### Save your marriage ahead of time

Nothing is guaranteed one hundred percent, but you can make your premarital agreement the best it can be. Communicate with your mate forthrightly. Hire a knowledgeable attorney; one who you can talk to so that you can explain your goals, and who gives you clear explanations so that you can use his advice. With love, premarital contracting works.

*Where do we begin talking this time?*
Your *whys* make your lover wise.

• Are you willing to work for your happiness?

*Discussion starter:*

• Where shall we store our premarital contracts once we sign
them?

For those of you who would like to do some additional reading on
the subject of this chapter:

*Family Law In A Nut Shell*, Harry D. Krause, Esq.
*Lindey on Separation Agreements and Antenuptial Contracts*, Volume 3,
Alexander Lindey; October 1989 Cumulative Supplement by Louis I.
Parley and Sarah D. Eldrich; April 1992 Cumulative Supplement by
Alexander Lindey and Louis I. Parley
*Love and the Law*, Gail J. Koff, Esq.
*Marriage, Divorce, Custody, & Living Together*, Steven Mitchell Sack
*Your Legal Guide to Marriage—and Other Relationships*, American Bar
Association, Public Education Division

# 11 *What Now?*

*Contracting: Now and forever for your healthy, happy, ongoing marriage.*

> For one human being to love another: that is perhaps the most difficult of all our tasks, the ultimate, the last test and proof, the work for which all other work is but preparation.
>
> RAINER MARIA RILKE

JAMES AND CYNTHIA stare into one another's eyes. His massive biceps flex as she sways in his arms. In a deep, but trembling voice, James asks, "Will you marry me?" Cynthia smiles; happy tears well in her eyes while she murmurs breathlessly, "Yes." Holding hands, they slowly walk into the sunset; silhouettes surrounded by pulsating sunbeams. The scene fades and the words "THE END" appear on the screen.

Many of us learn about love from romantic movies and other fantasies. We know that love leads us to the altar, but then what? Real life continues on—mundane days filled with work, cleaning, cooking meals, and taking care of children. How can partners keep their love alive each day?

## *Life goes on; so can loving partnerships*

We cannot always be alluring, calm, and rational. But with intimate contracting, lovers can express themselves, discuss their concerns, and solve their conflicts so that everyday and long-term issues don't smother their love. Continual use of premarital contracting builds communication muscles; even when we are feeling crazed, it helps us gear up for constructive interaction.

## *How can you keep love in your partnership?*

There are scores of preconceived notions, issues, concerns, and fears that mates bring to their relationship. Will your individual hang-ups and needs, submerged in the rush of romantic love, surface and take over once your Acute Romantic Phase passes after you marry? A woman's strength and independence, the very characteristics that her lover treasures, may have evolved due to insecurities caused by her past. Her self-doubt will surface now and again during their relationship, but that does not mean she isn't strong and independent too. A man's sensitive responsiveness to his partner, attributes that won him her heart, may have developed because of his fears of being abandoned. His neediness will emerge as their life together goes on, but he is still the empathetic person she fell in love with.

Premarital contracting helps lovers speak up about their needs. Then, through negotiation they can see which requirements are realistic, which are ghosts of the past, and which can be mutually accepted into their relationship. Once we marry, intimate contracting doesn't have to end; we can use it to stay connected and nourish our love for each other.

## *Communication is the key to happiness*

An issue that is too difficult to talk about before marriage, or a resistance by you or your lover to disclose yourself, may indicate difficulty ahead. We do not have to avoid sharing our thoughts.

Premarital contracting can lead lovers through a constructive communication process that helps them uncover and deal with problems. As time goes on we can become sure of our individual contracting techniques, and in our partner's willingness to listen to us and caringly respond. We will gain confidence in our ability to reach joint solutions. Our confidence in ourselves encourages yet more success and more love.

### Go into marriage with your eyes open

Premarital couples learn a lot about one another through their intimate contracting. Bob and I had no stress during our ARP. As our relationship matured and we adjusted to our daily routine, we had more fun and felt more love for each other. But our partnership hadn't been stretched by any problems. It wasn't until we had to figure out the more challenging of our premarital contracting issues that we began to learn how each of us handles our anxieties. Old fears, insecurities, and simple confusion because of our differing life experiences forced us to confront each other. It was wonderful. I was thrilled to find out that I liked the way Bob disagreed with me. Even when he was angry, he respected my space and gave me room to be myself. I tried to do the same for him.

We are both stubborn so our conversations were not always on an even keel, and often we had to get some distance from the particular issue we were talking about. Contracting was hard work for both of us, but we sure learned a lot about each other. Our premarital contracting also shortened the time it might have taken for us to build trust in our love. Now married for three years, when Bob and I have conflicts we can bring forth our intimate contracting skills—sooner or later. No one is perfect after all; nor do we have to be.

### Intimate contracting is a two-way street

The most important byway in your relationship is the route of responsive connection between you and your mate. Although it had been my idea to have a premarital contract, and initially Bob didn't see the need for one, once he knew my motives he contracted whole-heartedly. Actually, our discussions about why and why not to have a prenuptial agreement were our first, formal steps of premarital contracting. I could never have gone through the process if I had to fight Bob. His support and participation were my sustenance.

### But intimate contracting is hard!

Contracting requires tremendous give-and-take. That is not easy to do when you are in the grip of your emotions. Also, since our lives are full, it isn't always convenient to take the time to talk to our partners. Sometimes it can be almost *too* tempting to hope things go away. They don't. Finally, the most difficult part about contracting is gathering the fortitude you need to speak up for yourself, and to figure out how to communicate your thoughts so that you do not hurt your lover. It's worth it; facing issues keeps love healthy.

### I'm no fortune teller, but . . .

Hard-won solutions don't always remain relevant, and conditions change as our lives go on. What I can predict is that by using intimate contracting skills you will nourish your relationship. Experienced, premarital contracting couples become loving marriage partners. They know that communication takes time. Because they have confidence in their ability to talk to each other, they can keep from panicking when the going gets tough. They don't shut down their communication channels; they open them wider.

### Follow the yellow brick road

Joanna asks me, "How can I remember all the contracting techniques in your book? When Jeff and I are arguing, can I say, 'Wait a minute!', run for the book, and open it to my marked pages? Will I have to walk around with the book while we contract?" Bob and I need reminders too. It isn't possible to remember all the communication techniques we'd like to use while we are in the midst of contracting. But you and your partner can discuss the book together so that you develop a familiarity with intimate contracting techniques. The more you use your skills, the more they will calm your times of stress. You will recognize what your lover is trying to do, be less defensive, feel less disregarded, and more loved. When you use intimate contracting to support your communication, you are not trying to win over each other's losses, but win together so that your marriage stays a loving, solid relationship.

### What now?

You may have already completed many of your premarital contracting issues as you and your mate responded to the discussion questions at the end of each chapter. Now, you and your partner can decide how, or if you want to formalize the results of your premarital contracting. You can create prenuptial agreements that don't leave either of you hurt, but instead are covenants that encourage you to love each other more.

### Intimate contracting is never done

You may resolve your current issues, but new ones will evolve. Premarital contracting does not end; it transforms into marital contracting. Use your intimate contracting skills to stimulate and preserve your love.

# Sources
# for the
# Resourceful

## SERVE YOURSELF

All the questions lovers ask during their premarital contracting process cannot be predicted before hand, but knowing where to find
answers can be. The material in the Appendices of *Save Your
Marriage Ahead of Time* and the information at the end of each chapter can support lovers searching for tools to respond to their
questions.

# A SAMPLE PRENUPTIAL AGREEMENT

THIS AGREEMENT shall be effective as of the date the marriage is solemnized. This Agreement is between Diane L. Phillips ("Diane") and Jacob Travis ("Jake") (sometimes referred to collectively herein as "we" and "us").

## RECITALS

A. We intend to marry on 27 August 1989, and have been living together since October 1988 at a house owned by Diane in Bidwell, North Carolina. Diane has two daughters, Susan and Tracy, by a prior marriage. Jake has one son, Bill, by a prior marriage. We each want to preserve our abilities to provide for our children. We desire to define our financial rights and responsibilities.

B. Diane intends to make a transfer to Jake of a half interest in her Bidwell house, so that the marital home will be in both of our names as tenants by the entirety and to do this as a public symbol of our marriage. Notwithstanding the above, if our marriage is terminated before our fifth anniversary, the house ownership reverts to Diane. After that time we believe that Jake's contributions to the marital home will be such that he will have accrued equal ownership.

C. Diane, being one of three children, has received substantial gifts from her parents during her lifetime totaling over twenty-five-thousand dollars. She anticipates substantial inheritances from her parents.

D. Attached hereto as Exhibit A is a written statement of Diane's financial circumstances and current net worth as estimated to the best of her ability and signed by her. Diane's statement has been reviewed by Jake and he acknowledges that he has been provided with all information requested by him concerning Diane's assets, income and other financial circumstances, that he has been afforded ample opportunity to inquire and investigate further Diane's financial circumstances prior to the execution of this Agreement, and that after being afforded such opportunities, Jake waives his right to further inquiry, discovery and investigation. Jake expressly acknowledges that he is fully familiar with Diane's financial circumstances and that he is content with this Agreement.

E. Attached hereto as Exhibit B is a written statement of Jake's financial circumstances and current net worth as estimated to the best of his ability and signed by him. Jake's statement has been reviewed by Diane and she acknowledges that she has been provided with all information requested by her concerning Jake's assets, income and other financial circumstances, that she has been afforded ample opportunity to inquire and investigate further Jake's financial circumstances prior to the execution of this Agreement, and that after being afforded such opportunities, Diane waives her right to further inquiry, discovery and investigation. Diane expressly acknowledges that she is fully familiar with Jake's financial circumstances and that she is content with this Agreement.

F. It is our intention that notwithstanding our contemplated marriage, and irrespective of the place of such marriage or our present or future domicile, to make provision for one another in the event that we live separate and apart pursuant to court order from one another or are at some later time divorced.

G. It is further our intention, that upon the decease of either of us, the survivor shall have no right, title, interest or claim of any kind, statutory or otherwise, in or to the property or estate of the deceased, or to elect against the will of the other by reason of our marriage, except as hereinafter expressly set forth.

NOW THEREFORE, in consideration of the mutual promises hereinbelow set forth and our contemplated marriage, we hereto agree as follows:

1. Acknowledgment

We each acknowledge and agree that we are entering into this marriage out of love and affection for the other and without any desire or intention to demand or receive any benefits which would otherwise accrue to us by reason of this marriage for our support or in or to the other's property or as survivor upon the death of the other, except as hereinafter expressly set forth.

2. Confirmation

We each confirm our statements and waivers set forth in the Recitals above.

3. Pre-Marital Property

3.1. Separate Property. Each of us shall, during his or her lifetime, keep and retain sole ownership, enjoyment, control and power of disposition of all property owned by one of us to the exclusion of the other of every kind and nature whatsoever, owned at the time of the marriage (as evidenced by exhibits A and B attached hereto), free and clear of any interest, rights or claims of the other, including but not limited to, except as herein otherwise provided, any property into which same is converted, increments, accretions, or increases in value at any time of such assets, whether due to market conditions or the service, skills or efforts of either of us.

The real property wherein we presently reside, a house located at 101 Park Avenue, Bidwell, North Carolina, is, prior to the effective date of this Agreement, separate property belonging to Diane. As of the effective date of this Agreement, Diane transfers to Jake a half share in the Bidwell house, to be reflected in the title, so that the house will be held by us as tenants by the entirety, subject to distribution as set forth hereafter. Pursuant to paragraph 3.1., if our marriage is terminated before our fifth anniversary, the Bidwell house ownership reverts to Diane.

3.2. Interparty Gifts. Any gift or other gratuitous transfer from one of us to the other before the marriage, other than the transfer of interest in the Bidwell house, shall be treated and deemed the separate property of the donee and governed by paragraph 3.1. hereof.

3.3. Joint Property. Except as herein otherwise provided, any property owned jointly between us as of the time of the marriage shall remain in our joint ownership and shall be treated and deemed for the purposes hereof to have been acquired during the marriage and governed by paragraph 4.4 hereof. Such joint property does not now exceed one thousand dollars in value.

4. Property Acquired During the Marriage.

4.1. Separate Property. Any property acquired during the marriage in the name of one of us or under circumstances in which it is clear that such property was intended to be acquired separately by one of us or where the source of the funds or assets by which such separate property was acquired is pre-marital assets, shall remain the separate property of whoever of us acquires such assets, including but not limited to any property into which same is converted, increments, accretions or increases in value of such assets, whether due to market conditions or the services, skills or efforts of either of us.

4.2. Inheritance or Gifts from Third Parties. Any property acquired during the marriage by either of us by way of gift or inheritance from a third party shall be deemed the separate property of whoever of us so acquires it, including but not limited to any increments, accretions or increases in the value of such assets at any time thereto, whether due to market conditions or the services, skills or efforts of either of us. Any assets acquired by us as joint tenants or tenants by the entirety or tenants in common during the marriage by way of gift or inheritance from a third party shall be deemed joint property acquired during the marriage and governed by paragraph 4.4 hereof.

4.3. Interspousal Gifts. Any gift or other gratuitous transfers made by one of us to the other during the marriage shall be treated and deemed the separate property of the donee and such separate property shall include, but not be limited to, any property into which same is converted, increments, accretions or increases in value of such assets, whether due to market conditions or the services, skills or efforts of either of us, and such separate property shall be governed by paragraph 4.1 hereof.

4.4. Marital Property. Any property acquired during the marriage not deemed to be separate property under paragraph 4.1. or 4.2. hereof, or any other provision of this Agreement shall be treated and deemed to be joint assets acquired during the marriage.

5. Pre-Marital Debts

At the time of the execution of this Agreement, Diane has the debts which are listed in Exhibit A of this Agreement and Jake has the debts which are listed in Exhibit B of this Agreement, which debts shall be paid out of joint income as hereinafter defined.

6. Dedication of Income.

It is our intent that all the income we receive during the marriage while living together or prior to any action to dissolve our marital relationship, including dividend, rent or other income received or derived from separate property as defined herein, personal salaries, etc., shall be considered as joint income. In the event we separate or begin an action to dissolve our marital relationship, all such income from that day forward shall be for the benefit of the earner or owner of the separate property generating the income.

It is our intent, however, that any monies or property received as a result of the sale, conversion, increments, accretions, or increases in value of separate property as defined herein, shall not be considered joint income or joint property, but shall retain its character as separate property. Furthermore, the owner of separate property may change the nature of such property at will without regard to whether it effects the income-producing capacity of such property or changes it to non-income-producing property.

7. Termination of Marriage

    7.1. Definition of Term. The term "Termination of Marriage" shall mean the dissolution of the marriage by virtue of judicial proceedings by a court of competent jurisdiction rendering a judgment of divorce, annulment or other legal dissolution and shall also include a divorce from bed and board or other separation entered by a court of competent jurisdiction in a final order, judgment or decree.

    7.2. Alimony, Maintenance or Support. Each of us hereby expressly waives and relinquishes, during the marriage or in the event of separation or divorce or if the marriage is annulled, any and all rights to alimony, temporary or permanent spousal support, maintenance, counsel fees and expenses, and the right to use or occupy any real estate owned separately by the other or any claim to the separate property as defined herein of the other, by whatever name called, including, without limitation, any and all rights to alimony, maintenance or support pursuant to any existing statute, any amendment of or substitution therefor of any present or future statute, rule of court, custom or decision in North Carolina or in any other jurisdiction.

    7.3. Effect Upon Separate Property. We specifically acknowledge and agree that in the event of the termination of the marriage, each of us waives any and all right we may have to any interest or claim to the separate property of the other, as hereinbefore defined, including any right to future income from said separate property, including but not limited to dividends or rent.

    7.4. Effect Upon Interspousal Gifts. In the event of the termination of the marriage, any gifts from one of us to the other is separate property. Notwithstanding the above, the half interest in the Bidwell house transferred by Diane to Jake pursuant to paragraph 3.1. will revert to Diane's sole and exclusive ownership if the marriage terminates before Diane and Jake's fifth anniversary, after which time, if their marriage is terminated, the Bidwell house will be disposed according to paragraph 7.5.

7.5. Effect Upon Joint and/or Marital Property. It is our intention that in the event of the termination of the marriage before our fifth wedding anniversary, Diane shall receive sole and exclusive ownership of the Bidwell house, or if it has been sold, an amount equal to the net value received through the sale of the Bidwell house. After our fifth anniversary, the house and the remainder of the joint property, if any, shall be divided one-half to each of us.

7.6. Effect Upon Inheritances and Gifts from Third Parties. In the event of the termination of the marriage, each of us shall retain full and complete ownership of any gifts and/or inheritances either of us receive individually. Any gifts that we receive as joint tenants, tenants by the entirety, tenants in common or jointly in some other manner shall be divided equally one-half to each of us.


8. Our Deaths

Except as set forth herein, each of us hereby waives and relinquishes all rights that he or she may now have, or hereafter acquire, under present or future laws of any jurisdiction, of a share of the individual property in the estate of the other as a result of the marital relationship, including but not limited to dower, courtesy or any other right to take against the other's last will.

It is our further intention that all joint property shall become the property of the survivor.

In the event that we die at the same time, or if one of us dies within thirty days of the other, the joint property shall be divided equally one-half to each estate.


9. Consideration for Agreement

The consideration for this Agreement is the contemplated marriage between us and the mutual promises contained herein.


10. Effective Date

This Agreement shall become effective only when the contemplated marriage between us takes place, and if such marriage does not take place, this Agreement in all respects shall be null and void.

11. Waiver of Claims

11.1. Knowledge of Facts. We both acknowledge that we have each produced before the execution of this Agreement, in addition to the information set forth in Exhibits A and B hereof, financial statements, records and other documentation pertaining to our individual financial status, income, expenses, assets and liabilities. We each represent to the other the completeness, truthfulness and accuracy of said data, with the understanding that the other is relying thereon in accepting the terms contained herein and execution of this Agreement.

11.2. Voluntary Execution. We each represent that we have entered into this Agreement freely and voluntarily. We each further represent that we understand the meaning and effect of this Agreement and have fully discussed this Agreement with our respective attorneys.

11.3. Waiver of Property Rights. Except as herein to the contrary provided, each of us may dispose of our individual separate property in any way, and each of us hereby waives and relinquishes any and all right we may now have or hereafter acquire, under the present or future laws of any jurisdiction, to share in the property of the other as a result of the marital relationship, including, but not limited to, equitable distribution of property pursuant to North Carolina statutes or other statutory scheme for the division of marital property in any state where we reside or hold property.

11.4. Entire Agreement. This Agreement contains the entire understanding between us. There are no representations, warranties, promises, covenants, or understandings, oral or otherwise, direct or indirect, implicit or implied, other than those expressly set forth herein.

12. Judicial Proceedings

12.1. Non-collusive Agreement. It is expressly understood that, notwithstanding the provisions hereof, there have been no collusive agreements whatsoever, made either orally or in writing, or any representations by one of us to the other with respect to the procurement of a dissolution of the marriage, or restraining or inhibiting the other from contesting or litigating any proceedings which may be instituted one against the other in any matrimonial action at any time.

12.2. Incorporation of the Within Agreement. This Agreement shall be binding between us and the basis for judgment in any proceedings instituted by either of us in any court of competent jurisdiction in which a termination of the marriage is sought within the meaning of paragraph 7.1. hereof and shall be incorporated in any judgment rendered in that action.

12.3. Non-merger. Notwithstanding its incorporation in conformity with paragraph 12.2. into judgment terminating the marriage, entered by a court of competent jurisdiction, the provisions of this Agreement shall not merge with, but shall survive such judgment in its entirety, in full force and effect, except as may be invalidated by a court of competent jurisdiction in accordance with paragraph 12.4. hereof.

12.4. Severability. Should any provisions of this Agreement be held invalid or unenforceable by any court of competent jurisdiction, all other provisions shall, nonetheless, continue in full force and effect, to the extent that the remaining provisions are fair, just and equitable.

12.5. Modification or Waiver. No modification or waiver of any of the terms of this Agreement shall be valid unless in writing and executed by the one of us to be charged. The failure of either of us to insist upon strict performance of any of the provisions of this Agreement shall not be deemed a waiver of any subsequent breach or default of any provision contained in this Agreement.

13. General Provisions

13.1. Independent Counsel. We each acknowledge that we have retained separate and independent counsel of our own choosing and that we have been separately and independently advised regarding every aspect of this agreement. Diane was represented by John Smith, Jr., Esq. Jake was represented by Jane Doe, Esq.

13.2. Preparation of Agreement. We have chosen to prepare this Agreement ourselves with guidance from both our counsels.

13.3. Further Documents. We each respectively agree that we will, at any time hereafter, on request, make, execute and deliver any and all deeds, releases, waivers, and other instruments, papers or documents as the other may reasonably require for the purpose of giving full effect to the covenants, provisions, promises and terms contained within this Agreement, including but not limited to any documents specifically provided for herein.

13.4. Situs. The laws of the State of North Carolina shall govern the execution and enforcement of this Agreement.

13.5. Original Agreements. This Agreement shall be executed in four counterparts, two for each of us, and each counterpart shall be the Agreement with the same effect as any other counterpart.

13.6. Survivorship. This Agreement shall inure to the benefit of each of us and our heirs

13.7. Headings. The headings of several subdivisions and paragraphs of this agreement are inserted solely for the convenience of reference and shall have no further meaning, force or affect.

EXHIBIT A

DIANE L. PHILLIPS

**Assets**

| | |
|---|---|
| Residence | $252,600 |
|     101 Park Avenue | |
|     Bidwell, North Carolina | |
|     Legal description | |
|     Value from 10/1/88 tax bill | |
| Building | 45,000 |
|     4561 Tyler Road | |
|     Bidwell, North Carolina | |
|     Legal Description | |
|     Appraised 7/14/88 | |
| Limited Partnership shares: | 13,750 |
| IRA Account (6/29/88) | 11,787 |
| Brokerage Account (6/26/87) | 31,422 |
| Money Market (6/30/87) | 4,363 |
| Bonds: (Face values as of dates shown): | |
|     County of. . . . (due 7/1/92) | 5,000 |
|     City of. . . . (due 9/1/93) | 5,000 |
|     State of. . . . (due 9/1/98) | 5,000 |
|     Municipal Agency. . . . (due 1/1/20) | 5,000 |
|     Municipal Agency. . . . (due 1/1/22) | 5,000 |
| Personal Jewelry and household belongings | |
|     appraised 8/8/80 for insurance purposes | 25,000 |
| 1981 Volvo purchased in 1987 | 8,000 |

**Liabilities**

| | |
|---|---|
| Home Improvement Loan | 13,000 |

EXHIBIT B

JACOB TRAVIS

**Assets**
Land: 20 acres
    Bidwell, North Carolina ('88 tax bill)        $ 47,392
    1980 Saab (1986 purchase price)        7,750
    Personal and household goods (est.)        10,000

**Liabilities**
Personal note to friend        7,000

IN PRESENCE OF:

_____    _____
                                 Diane L. Phillips

_____    _____
                                 Dated

_____    _____
                                 Jacob Travis

_____    _____
                                 Dated

STATE OF NORTH CAROLINA
BENTON COUNTY, SS.

On this _____ day of August, 1989, before me personally appeared Diane L. Phillips, to me known and known to me to be the person who signed her name to the within Instrument, and acknowledged to me that she signed same of her free act and deed and gave oath to the truth therein.

_____
Notary Public

STATE OF NORTH CAROLINA
BENTON COUNTY, SS.

On this _____ day of August, 1989, before me personally appeared Jacob Travis, to me known and known to me to be the person who signed his name to the within Instrument, and acknowledged to me that he signed same of his free act and deed and gave oath to the truth therein.

_____
Notary Public

# B UNIFORM PREMARITAL AGREEMENT ACT

## Section 1. Definitions

As used in this Act:
(1) "Premarital agreement" means an agreement between prospective spouses made in contemplation of marriage and to be effective upon marriage.
(2) "Property" means an interest, present or future, legal or equitable, vested or contingent, in real or personal property, including income and earnings.

## Section 2. Formalities

A premarital agreement must be in writing and signed by both parties. It is enforceable without consideration.

## Section 3. Content

(a) Parties to a premarital agreement may contract with respect to:
    (1) the rights and obligations of each of the parties in any of the property of either or both of them whenever and wherever acquired or located;
    (2) the right to buy, sell, use, transfer, exchange, abandon, lease, consume, expend, assign, create a security interest in, mortgage, encumber, dispose of, or otherwise manage and control property;

    (3)  the disposition of property upon separation, marital dissolution, death, or the occurrence or nonoccurrence of any other event;

    (4)  the modification or elimination of spousal support;

    (5)  the making of a will, trust, or other arrangement to carry out the provisions of the agreement;

    (6)  the ownership rights in and disposition of the death benefit from a life insurance policy;

    (7)  the choice of law governing the construction of the agreement; and

    (8)  any other matter, including their personal rights and obligations, not in violation of public policy or a statute imposing a criminal penalty.

(b)    The right of a child to support may not be adversely affected by a premarital agreement.

## Section 4. Effect of Marriage

A premarital agreement becomes effective upon marriage.

## Section 5. Amendment, Revocation

After marriage, a premarital agreement may be amended or revoked only by a written agreement signed by the parties. The amended agreement or the revocation is enforceable without consideration.

## Section 6. Enforcement

(a)    A premarital agreement is not enforceable if the party against whom enforcement is sought proves that:

    (1)  that party did not execute the agreement voluntarily; or

    (2)  the agreement was unconscionable when it was executed and, before execution of the agreement, that party:

        (i)   was not provided a fair and reasonable disclosure of the property or financial obligations of the other party;

        (ii)  did not voluntarily and expressly waive, in writing, any right to disclosure of the property or financial obligations of the other party beyond the disclosure provided; and

        (iii) did not have, or reasonably could not have had, an adequate knowledge of the property or financial obligations of the other party.

(b) If a provision of a premarital agreement modifies or eliminates spousal support and that modification or elimination causes one party to the agreement to be eligible for support under a program of public assistance at the time of separation or marital dissolution, a court, notwithstanding the terms of the agreement, may require the other party to provide support to the extent necessary to avoid that eligibility.

(c) An issue of unconscionability of a premarital agreement shall be decided by the court as a matter of law.

## Section 7. Enforcement: Void Marriage

If a marriage is determined to be void, an agreement that would otherwise have been a premarital agreement is enforceable only to the extent necessary to avoid an inequitable result.

## Section 8. Limitation of Actions

Any statute of limitations applicable to an action asserting a claim for relief under a premarital agreement is tolled during the marriage of the parties to the agreement. However, equitable defenses limiting the time for enforcement, including laches and estoppel, are available to either party.

## Section 9. Application and Construction

This [Act] shall be applied and construed to effectuate its general purpose to make uniform the law with respect to the subject of this [Act] among states enacting it.

## Section 10. Short Title

This [Act] may be cited as the Uniform Premarital Agreement Act.

## Section 11. Severability

If any provision of this [Act] or its application to any person or circumstance is held invalid, the invalidity does not affect other provisions or applications of this [Act] which can be given effect without the invalid provision or application, and to this end the provisions of this [Act] are severable.

## Section 12. Time of Taking Effect

This [Act] takes effect _____ and applies to any premarital agreement executed on or after that date.

## Section 13. Repeal

The National Conference of Commissioners on Uniform State Laws has also written the *Uniform Marital Property Act*, which is a rich source of ideas for premarital contracting couples. Although this act is too extensive to include in this book, copies may be obtained (for a nominal fee) from:

National Conference of Commissioners on Uniform State Laws
676 North St. Clair Street
Suite 1700
Chicago, IL 60611
(312) 915-0195

You can read the *Uniform Marital Property Act* ("UMPA"), in county law libraries, which are open to the public; law school libraries, many of which are also open to the public; and some local libraries. At the libraries, copies of the Act will be located in such looseleaf services as Matthew Bender, Commerce Clearing House ("CCH"), and Prentice-Hall. Two other places to look for the Act are the *Family Reporter* published by the Bureau of National Affairs and the *Uniform Laws Annotated* by West Publishing Company. Your Family Law attorney may have a copy of "UMPA" for you to refer to as well.

The *Uniform Marital Property Act* and the *Uniform Premarital Agreement Act* have been approved by the American Bar Association. Has your state adopted these acts?

The National Conference of Commissioners on Uniform State Laws has given permission for the inclusion of the *Uniform Premarital Agreement Act* in this book.

# C THE IDEAL SCHEDULE FOR PRENUPTIAL AGREEMENT

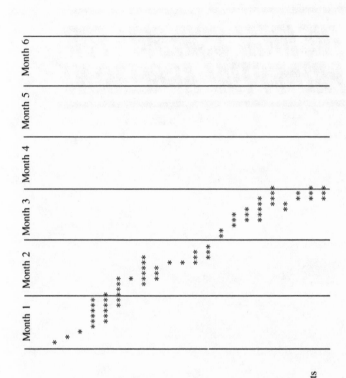

| | Month 1 | Month 2 | Month 3 | Month 4 | Month 5 | Month 6 |
|---|---|---|---|---|---|---|
| · Make mutual commitment to contract | * | | | | | |
| · Begin dialogue with yourself | ** | | | | | |
| · Begin dialogue with your partner | *** | | | | | |
| · Identify individual and joint issues | ****** | | | | | |
| · Discuss your concerns and dreams | ****** | | | | | |
| · Think of ways to achieve your goals | ****** | | | | | |
| · Begin search for experts | * | | | | | |
| · Continue contracting, write ideas down | ****** | | | | | |
| · Interview experts | *** | | | | | |
| · Choose experts | | * | | | | |
| · Hire independent legal counsel | | *** | | | | |
| · Determine what experts need from you | | *** | | | | |
| · Prepare information for experts | | ** | | | | |
| · Hold first meetings with experts | | *** | | | | |
| · Contract options suggested by experts | | ***** | | | | |
| · Write options out | | ***** | | | | |
| · Develop detailed options with experts | | *** | | | | |
| · Negotiate options with your partner | | ** | | | | |
| · Review material with both attorneys | | ** | | | | |
| · Negotiate with your partner | | *** | | | | |
| · Design solutions with partner and experts | | ** | | | | |
| · Write out options | | ** | | | | |

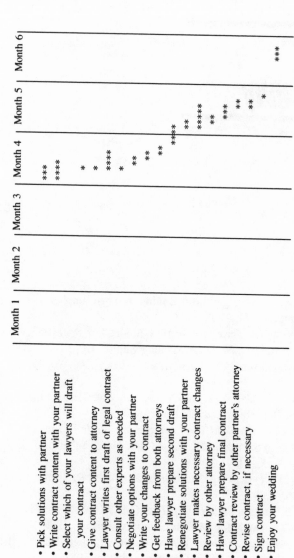

| | Month 1 | Month 2 | Month 3 | Month 4 | Month 5 | Month 6 |
|---|---|---|---|---|---|---|
| Pick solutions with partner | | | | *** | | |
| Write contract content with your partner | | | | **** | | |
| Select which of your lawyers will draft your contract | | | | * | | |
| Give contract content to attorney | | | | * | | |
| Lawyer writes first draft of legal contract | | | | **** | | |
| Consult other experts as needed | | | | * | | |
| Negotiate options with your partner | | | | ** | | |
| Write your changes to contract | | | | ** | | |
| Get feedback from both attorneys | | | | ** | | |
| Have lawyer prepare second draft | | | | **** | | |
| Renegotiate solutions with your partner | | | | ** | | |
| Lawyer makes necessary contract changes | | | | ***** | | |
| Review by other attorney | | | | | ** | |
| Have lawyer prepare final contract | | | | | *** | |
| Contract review by other partner's attorney | | | | | ** | |
| Revise contract, if necessary | | | | | ** | |
| Sign contract | | | | | * | |
| Enjoy your wedding | | | | | | *** |

Life is not perfect or ideal. If you have less than six months until your wedding, you can still go for it!

Respect yourselves and be fair to each other

# Bibliography

*Black's Law Dictionary*; Abridged Fifth Edition; Henry Campbell Black; West Publishing Co.; St. Paul; 1983

"Contractual Ordering Of Marriage: A New Model For State Policy"; *California Law Review*; Marjorie Maguire Shultz, Esq.; Boalt Hall School of Law, University of California, Berkeley; Vol. 70, No. 2; March 1982

*Contracts*; Gordon D. Schaber, Esq. and Claude D. Rohwer, Esq.; Nutshell Series of West Publishing Co.; St. Paul; 1990

*Don't Get Married Until You Read This: A Layman's Guide To Prenuptial Agreements*; David Saltman, J.D., L.L.M. and Harry Schaffner, J.D.; Barron's; New York; 1989

*Family Law*; Harry D. Krause, Esq.; Nutshell Series of West Publishing Co.; St. Paul; 1986

*Getting Together: Building a Relationship That Gets To Yes*; Roger Fisher and Scott Brown; Houghton Mifflin Company; Boston; 1988

*Getting To Yes: Negotiating Agreement Without Giving In*; Roger Fisher and William Ury; Houghton Mifflin Company; Boston; 1981

"How Effective Is Marriage Preparation?", David H. Olson, Ph.D.; *Prevention In Family Services: Approaches To Family Wellness*; David Mace (Ed.); Sage Publications; Beverly Hills; 1983

*Husbands and Wives: Exploding Marital Myths/Deepening Love and Desire*;
  Dr. Melvyn Kinder and Dr. Connell Cowan; Clarkson N. Potter, Inc./
  Publisher; 1989

*Intimate Strangers: Men and Women Together*; Lillian B. Rubin; Harper &
  Row, Publishers, Inc.; New York; 1982

*Justice, Gender and The Family*; Susan Moller Okin; Basic Books, Inc.,
  Publishers; New York; 1989

*Law Dictionary*; Second Edition; Steven H. Gifis; Barron's Educational
  Series, Inc.; New York; 1984

*Lindey On Separation Agreements and Antenuptial Contracts*; October 1989
  Cumulative Supplement by Louis I. Parley, Esq. and Sarah D. Eldrich,
  Esq.; Matthew Bender; Times Mirror Books

*Love and Money*; Sylvia Porter; William Morrow and Company Inc.; New
  York; 1985

*Love And The Law*; Gail J. Koff, Esq.; Simon and Schuster; New York; 1989

*Love Is Never Enough*; Aaron T. Beck, M.D.; Harper & Row, Publishers;
  New York; 1989

*Make Your Own Contract: Simple Contracts For Personal Use*; Stephen
  Elias, Esq.; Nolo Press; Berkeley; 1990

*Male Survival: Masculinity without Myth*; Harvey E. Kaye M.D.; Grosset
  & Dunlap; New York; 1974

*Man's World, Woman's Place: A Study in Social Mythology*; Elizabeth
  Janeway; William Morrow and Company, Inc.; New York; 1971

*Marriage And The Family In The Middle Ages*; Frances and Joseph Gies;
  Harper & Row, Publishers; New York; 1987

*Marriage, Divorce, Custody, & Living Together*; Steven Mitchell Sack;
  Fisher Books; 1987

*Men/Women Issues In Human Development*; Peggy Natiello, Ph.D.; Private
  circulation

*More Equal Than Others: Women and Men in Dual-Career Marriages*;
  Rosanna Hertz; University of California Press; Berkeley; 1986

*One Of The Guys: The Wising Up Of An American Man*; Harry Stein; Simon
  and Schuster; New York; 1988

*People Skills*; Robert Bolton, Ph.D.; Touchstone, Simon and Schuster; New
  York; 1986

*Perfect Women: Hidden Fears of Inadequacy and The Drive To Perform*;
  Colette Dowling; Summit Books; New York; 1988

*Premarital Agreements*; Joseph P. Zwack; Harper & Row, Publishers; New
  York; 1987

"Prenuptial Agreements: A Time For A Change In Public Policy"; George F. Bearup, Esq.; *Michigan Bar Journal*; October 1989

*Second Shift: Working Parents And The Revolution At Home*; Arlie Hochschild, with Anne Machung; Viking Penguin Inc.; New York; 1989

"Some Differences Between Men And Women"; Ethel S. Person; *The Atlantic Monthly*; March 1988

*The Art of Negotiating: Psychological Strategies For Gaining Advantageous Bargains*; Gerard I. Nierenberg; Hawthorn Books, Inc.; New York; 1968

*The Divorce Revolution*; Lenore J. Weitzman; The Free Press, Macmillan, Inc.; New York; 1985

*The Feminine Mystique*; Betty Friedan; W.W. Norton & Company, Inc.; New York; 1983

*The Future of Marriage*; Jessie Bernard; World Publishing Company; New York; 1972

*The Inner Male: Overcoming Roadblocks To Intimacy*; Herb Goldberg, Ph.D.; New American Library; New York; 1987

*The Law of Sex Discrimination*; Professor of Philosophy J. Ralph Lindgren and Professor of Law Nadine Taub; West Publishing Company; St. Paul, Minnesota; 1988

*The Making Of The Modern Family*; Edward Shorter; Basic Books, Inc.; New York; 1975

*The Marriage Bargain: Women and Dowries In European History*; Marion A. Kaplan, Ed.; Harrington Park Press; New York; 1985

*The Marriage Contract: Spouses, Lovers, and the Law*; Lenore J. Weitzman; The Free Press, a Division of Macmillan Publishing Co., Inc.; New York; 1981

*The Mirages of Marriage*; William J. Lederer, and Don D. Jackson, M.D.; W.W. Norton & Company, Inc.; New York; 1968

*The New Male-Female Relationship*; Herb Goldberg, Ph.D.; William Morrow and Company, Inc.; New York; 1983

*The Underside of History: A View of Women Through Time*; Dr. Elise Boulding; Westview Press; Boulder, Colorado; 1976

*Toward A New Psychology of Women*; Jean Baker Miller, M.D.; Second Edition; Beacon Press; Boston; 1986

*Women And Home-Based Work: The Unspoken Contract*; Kathleen Christensen; Henry Holt and Company; New York; 1988

*Women's Reality: An Emerging Female System in a White Male Society*;

Anne Wilson Schaef; Perennial Library, Harper & Row, Publishers; San Francisco; 1981

*Your Legal Guide To Marriage—and Other Relationships*; American Bar Association, Public Education Division; You and the Law Series; 1989

*Your Perfect Right*; Robert E. Alberti, Ph.D. and Michael L. Emmons, Ph.D.; Impact; California; 1970

LIBRARY
ST. LOUIS COMMUNITY COLLEGE
AT FLORISSANT VALLEY